SMART STOCKS

THE INSIGHTFUL BOOK FOR INTELLIGENT INVESTORS

JEFF LUKE

DEDICATION

This book is dedicated to my parents, Michael and Renee, for providing so many opportunities in life and for encouraging my creativity.

CONTENTS

Quote   vii
Foreword   ix
Introduction   xvii

1. Temperament   1
2. Identify   10
3. Talent   27
4. A Sensible Price   45
5. No   60
6. Invest   75
7. Understanding   90
8. Moat   107
9. How to Read an Annual Report   129
10. Anatomy and Dissection of a 10-K   135
11. Putting It All Together   154
12. Hope Stocks Will Get Cheap   173
13. Get Ready to Buy Stocks   175
14. How to Buy Stocks   178
15. Let's Not Party Like It's 1999   181

Afterword   185
Thank you   187
Connect   189
Acknowledgments   191
Disclaimer   193
Notes   195
About the Author   203

"I'M ALWAYS DOING THINGS I CANNOT DO, THAT'S HOW I GET TO DO THEM." — PICASSO

FOREWORD

It started in French class

    We moved to Newton, Massachusetts when I was about 12. I had a new school and new teachers, and when it came time to picking foreign language class, I chose French. I lucked out because I got a great teacher I'll never forget, Mr. Price. He made always found a way to link what we learned about the language to French culture, like bringing freshly-baked almond, chocolate, and ham & cheese croissants to class so we could get appreciate the best parts of French culture. We never heard him use English words in that class. Not a single word.

    The best part of class was when Mr. Price taught us how to express human emotions. When describing "I'm afraid" he would climb under his desk whimpering in fear. For "I'm hungry" he would mime hunger, and the same for thirsty, happy, sad, etc. He put one hundred percent into acting out every emotion, and now, decades later, I still remember every phrase.

    I admire his teaching to this day, not only for the memorable acting, but also because he gave us this great framework to learn verbs and phrases. It was so simple and complete—he'd turn every conjugation into a rap or a song—that it's as easy to recall today as it was when I first learned them.

In the years since it has been so much easier to learn Spanish and Portuguese because the framework is there, and the learning method is solid. I was able to learn enough Portuguese to go down to Brazil on my own and live there for six months, traveling all over the country, and I don't think it would have been easy to do if my early language learning foundation had not been so solid.

I'm fortunate to have had terrific teachers, and I want to return the gift they've given me by sharing what I've learned with you.

Learning about stocks

Learning a new language is actually a lot like learning to invest. First, you learn a new word and you practice saying it until it sounds right. Then you learn another new word, and before you know it you can string a few words together into a phrase.

In that same way, you begin investing when you buy your first stock. Then you buy another stock, and another. Before you know it, you've collected a few stocks and now you have something called a "portfolio".

It's very easy to get started in trading, but it's an entirely different thing to do it successfully and for a long time. The goal of investing is to get more money in the future in return for the money you invest today. Many people who think they're investing properly are in reality gambling or hoping things will work out, and they wind up losing a lot of money.

Breaking down my language learning

Allow me to break down my language-learning process for you. I like to spend 3-6 months learning things naturally. I like to learn a few basic phrases, the "Legos of language" if you will, and just practice those until I know them. The phrases you need in any language are similar. You need to know how to say "this" and "that" and also how to say "I want" or "I would like" and then some nouns like "water" or "restaurant" or "beer" are also pretty handy as well.

I don't know how to learn a language through grammar, or learning subjects and verbs and objects and direct objects, and I'm not skilled in making sentence diagrams. If you think of how you learned to speak your first language, it was initially through simple words and then learning how to connect them into phrases and questions. Much of your learning was in speaking with other people, or singing songs, or looking at pictures in books and naming what you saw.

When I'm learning a new language I take my time and have fun, often listening to songs in other languages. I like to get the lyrics to the songs and follow along with them. When I was teaching myself Brazilian Portuguese my CD player was filled with Brazilian music singers and I sang along. I had a dictionary nearby to look up all the new words I heard in the song and I also got recordings of language lessons and listened to them while I was driving the car. I like getting picture books and magazines in the new language as well, doing my best to approach learning with a beginner's mind. Today, I learn a lot by watching YouTube and listening to podcasts in any language I want to learn.

Then, after all that, I like to practice with native speakers; speaking only in that language, trying hard not to cheat, even one minute, as the brain needs to bathe in the sounds of the new language and switching to English only thwarts progress. Going to the country is an enormous advantage as well, especially when one travels away from the hotels and other English speakers. Total immersion leads to rapid fluency. Intelligence is not required, only the ability to work within a framework, to take your time to learn, and to focus your attention on your goal for 3-6 months is essential. Most people I know who are perpetually trying to learn new languages lack that kind of focus. They could have it, but it's all too easy to get distracted these days.

"Close the door and make the cart"

There's a Chinese idiom, "bì mén zào chē," which translates to "close the door and build the cart." I love this idiom because it conveys the idea of being self-taught, as in shutting yourself in your ivory tower, isolated from the demanding world, and getting something done.

That's how I learned to invest, after all. I'm a self-taught investor—I have never taken a business class, yet when I started investing I knew that I could focus my attention and learn on my own. After Malcolm Gladwell's prescribed 10,000 hours of reading, studying, and practicing, I like to think I've become a halfway decent investor, to say the least

But now I'm here because I want to show you everything that I've learned as a self-taught investor in the hopes that I can save you from years of frustration and investing dollars needlessly going down the drain.

I started investing at 26

I started investing when I was 26. Back then I was just starting my career as a professional photographer and I was totally on my own. I was starting out in business for myself and the future seemed terrifying and uncertain.

Somewhere along the road, though, I started to read more about investing. I had the good luck to be living and photographing in Seattle, and I was just starting my business at the same time Jeff Bezos was starting Amazon. It was an exciting time for me as I started to get a lot of professional photography gigs, and every month I was able to save just enough extra money to put aside to invest and grow for the future.

Soon I met someone named Herb Bridge, he gave me his card. Herb's family owned Ben Bridge Jewelers, a business with 65 stores stretching from Washington to California. Every few months I would mail Herb and about 30 other people I'd met during my photo shoots in downtown Seattle a postcard featuring one of my photos—it was one of the ways I let people know about my portrait photography. He would always call after receiving my postcard and thank me for thinking of him, and he would explain that his kids where grown up and they were in charge of photos of the grandchildren. "I wish you all the best with your photography—you certainly deserve it," he once said.

I was reading the Berkshire Hathaway annual report one year—it was kind of like a sport for me; someone said you should read Warren Buffett's letter to shareholders as a great education to investing. It was easy enough to download the letter off the website and read it, and in May of 2000 I remember reading that Berkshire Hathaway had bought Ben Bridge Jeweler, and in the Berkshire Hathaway Chairman's Letter Buffett wrote, "In their typically classy way, the Bridges allocated a substantial portion of the proceeds from their sale to the hundred of co-workers who had helped the company achieve its success."

I thought to myself, "The Bridges *are* classy!" Herb Bridge would call me every time he received one of my postcards just to thank me for thinking of him and to give me his best wishes. And now here was this fabulously successful diamond businessman, and he took the time to encourage a photographer who was just starting out.

I decided to write a letter to Buffett letting him know I agreed with him about the Bridges, and to tell him how kind and encouraging Herb had been over the years. I sent the letter Buffett at Berkshire Hathaway, and a week letter I got a letter from Warren Buffett himself! He thanked me for writing and shared a few humorous observations about something I wrote. I framed the letter.

Then a few months passed and I returned home one day to a voicemail message. It was Herb Bridge, and he said that he'd just been to Bill Gates' house for the annual CEO summit. While he was there, he saw Warren Buffett, who gave him a photocopy of my letter. "That was a really sweet thing you did, writing that letter," Herb said on the recording. "Thank you so much. I wish you all the best."

A year or so later, Warren Buffett returned to Seattle and I was lucky enough to be invited to meet him and take some photos. It was a special day, finally having the chance to meet someone I'd learned so much about. He was every bit as cheerful, funny, and friendly as I had heard, and yes, he really loves Cherry Coke. It was a huge milestone in my life. I got to meet the greatest living investor, one of those rare opportunities in life that happens once and deserves to be cherished.

Starting in the early 2000s, I began to roll up my sleeves and start learning about stocks. I still invested in mutual funds, but the challenge of learning about the specific companies that these superstar managers were buying was exciting. How do you know which stocks to buy? It was a big question, and I had no answers. There was a lot of guess work and a little bit of buying and hoping (more like praying). I had no real guide, even though you could Google everything and learn on your own. But I did the best I could and eventually bought a few stocks.

My first few attempts were... uninspiring. Without knowing what to look for, it was really mostly what I'd call "rearview" investing. I was looking at companies that had done well in the past, and bought some shares hoping that the stellar performance would continue. I assure you, it did not.

Looking back, I realized that I didn't truly understand the stocks I was buying. I was buying them because some rockstar fund manager bought them or because the brand name was famous, so I thought the stock must be great. But the truth is, my first three stocks (GE, Intel, and Pfizer) were not good ideas. I bought the first two after their stock had been on a great run, and they suffered after. Pfizer turned out to be a stock whose price went nowhere for years.

Finally I bought a stock that made sense. I bought shares of Berkshire Hathaway. It made sense because I had been reading the company's annual report for quite a while, and I understood the company well. So I saved up enough money to buy a few of the less expensive "B" shares and then bought as many as I could. It was one of the best investments I ever made, and I still own every share to this day.

Buffett is a great teacher, and he doesn't have to help people as much as he does. He truly is an artist in that he shares his creative work with other people.

Most people think he's just an investor and businessman, but he spends a lot of his time traveling the country and talking to students about investing. He could, of course, just be some rich guy sitting back by the pool with all his money, but he is generous and spends his time connecting with people, "investing" in our youth, you could say.

How to start stock investing

You can easily set up a brokerage account to trade stocks on your computer or smartphone. Once you've set up your account, which might take a day or two to become official, you can buy or sell stocks. Some brokerage firms charge a fee of $7 or so, while others like Robinhood, Schwab, and TD Ameritrade now offer free stock trades; this was unheard of just three short years ago.

The mechanics of investing are simple and becoming easier every day. The problem is that many beginning investors have no useful framework to evaluate potential stocks. The ordinary investor who is actively trading is going to get mediocre or bad results—much worse than the market provides. Trading based on emotions of fear and greed, and the high taxes you have to pay on short-term gains will eat into profits. This underscores the importance of being patient, buying when opportunities arrive, and buying stocks in companies you understand.

If investing is so hard, why read this book?

You read a book like this because you want to get smart, and there are few better ways to accumulate wisdom than through reading.

One nice side-effect of gaining wisdom about investing is that if you do it right you can get rich. You won't get rich fast, so let me dissuade you of that silly notion right now. But if you're like me you'll enjoy the pursuit of learning about different companies, because each has its own story and it's constantly changing. So as you follow different companies you're witnessing the dynamics of changing narratives, and you also have a chance to "buy in" to some of these great companies if you're ready when opportunities arrive.

Think about this for a moment: most people who speak English as their mother tongue don't need to learn other languages. Most people don't need to get better at basketball, golf or tennis unless it's their job. Investing is a similar pursuit, in that you don't have to invest. People who get good at investing tend to enjoy the process and they keep at it, not because they need more money, but because they enjoy learning, reading, and applying new ideas.

Also, you might turn out to have a talent at investing, and you won't know unless you give it a try. Ben Franklin said, "Hide not your Talents, they for Use were made. What's a Sun-Dial in the shade!"

This book provides the framework for making investing enjoyable and productive, and giving the reader a fluency that they can improve on with time and practice.

INTRODUCTION

Happy families are all alike

Leo Tolstoy's novel Anna Karenina begins: "Happy families are all alike; every unhappy family is unhappy in its own way." In the same way, happy businesses are all alike; they have similar patterns of success, and your job is to identify them. I will show you how.

The tools in this book will help you to recognize the patterns of these happy families of business. Many of the stocks out there are not worth your time, but you can learn to recognize the patterns that lead you to identify outstanding businesses so you can buy their stocks and pass by the others.

Don't follow "common sense" advice

If you believe that you can invest, I know you can do it. I'm here to encourage and educate you. You've probably heard a lot of advice about investing, and much of it is bullshit.

You're told a lot of advice is "common sense," but I think the common condition is ignorance and stupidity. If you want to do better than the crowd you need to do *uncommon* things.

Let me just give you a quick example: You must be patient to be a great investor. I'm not saying to just be average, but to be the kind of investor I believe you can be. For example, I've purchased one new stock (it was Amazon) in the last seven years. I waited until I understood the business and it was cheap. Now, most investors need to constantly be "doing" something, even when there are not good opportunities. You want stocks to be cheap, and you have to have your eyes wide open when the moment arrives and have cash available. Finally, you have to have the courage to buy when others are selling, which is contrary to what most people do. Like I said, you have to do uncommon things.

Imagine for a moment that you decided to hire a stock broker or other professional to help you pick stocks and they tell you it might take five years to pick a fantastic stock selling at the right price. You'd walk right out the door! Nobody has that kind of time to wait.

I don't think you'll have to wait five years to find your next investment, but I do believe that you have your own best interests in mind. Investment advisers only get paid if you buy stuff, they get paid for action. But nobody has to pay you to sit around and wait if you don't have a good opportunity.

Also, stocks have been expensive, for the most part, for the past several years. What I mean by that is that nobody who has just been investing for the past 10 years knows what a market decline is like, and people will freak out when it happens. It may sound scary right now to buy stocks when everyone is losing their mind, but that's where you make money.

Most people will be better off investing in an S&P 500 index fund because they don't have to think about stocks. I'd say 98% or 99% of investors, and this is because most people just don't have the time or desire to spend reading about, analyzing and valuing businesses. They just want to own a part of the businesses of the United States, and they're happy with the decent returns they will get. That's a perfectly good route for most people who want to "know nothing" about stocks to take.

For the enterprising investor who wants to bring some intensity to the game, there are steps you can take to improve your chances of success. I want to educate you so you'll understand the temperament and understanding required for success.

The mere fact that you're reading this book suggests that you are not interested in being a sheep and following the herd. When stocks get popular and everyone is buying the same things stock prices get too high, and eventually markets crash. People sell in a panic and stocks get cheap. That is when you want to buy stocks in outstanding companies. This book will help you identify those companies so you'll be prepared when opportunities arrive. Here are a few important concepts you'll discover.

The keys to successful investing:

1. You don't need a diversified portfolio
2. You don't need a financial adviser
3. Don't pay attention to market forecasts
4. Don't fear stock market crashes
5. Don't have a cavalier attitude about losing money
6. Never confuse speculation with investing
7. Only invest in companies you understand

Bring intensity to the game

For most investors, about 99% of the people who want to invest should diversify and not buy individual stocks, and they will be well served with a very low cost index fund. They'll be much better off making a decision to own a broad collection of American companies; that makes a lot of sense, and that is the way they should approach investing.

Now, if you want to invest to get much better returns than the rest of the world you have to bring an *intensity* to the game. You have to decide to evaluate businesses before you buy their stocks, and that requires extra effort and intensity and time to get that job done. Once you decide to do this I think diversification is a terrible mistake.

Investing vs. gambling

Right out of the gates I want to make a distinction between investing and gambling.

With *investing*, you buy a productive asset — it could be an apartment complex, a farm, or stock in a company like Apple — that you expect to generate profits year after year.

With *gambling*, you buy an asset with the hope that you can sell it to someone else at a higher price. The asset itself does not create anything. For example, if you buy a gold coin, it just sits there and does nothing. You can stroke or touch or caress it, but it's just a piece of gold, and you can only hope to sell it to someone else at a higher price. The same goes for a painting, a pair of rare Nikes or bitcoin[1] — they do not generate cash over time. Unlike a farm or a car dealership or an apartment complex, the price is based on what someone else will pay for it.

People are fascinated with the idea they can "get rich quick" and would rather take huge risks with gambles to double their money in six months. That's why people go to Vegas, buy lottery tickets, etc. They know the odds are against them, and they still do it. There's a strong instinct to want to get rich fast, and I don't know how to do it. I see people putting a lot of money into speculative stocks and high-priced IPOs and even thought they think they're investing, it's all about wanting that stock price to go up; it's not about the *business* - it's all about the *price*, and that's gambling.

When you want to invest, ask yourself if the underlying business is profitable. If the company has been around long enough to establish a solid track record then it may be a predictable business worth your investment. If it's not profitable yet and you're just hoping one day it will be (Tesla, Uber, etc) then it's a gamble. The world is full of foolish gamblers and they won't do as well as investors who bring an intensity to the game of investing long term.

I watch a lot of financial YouTubers and follow several other investment channels on the platform. Every now and then I even engage on Reddit. One thing, though, that really surprises me is the number of people who teach viewers ways to get rich quickly in the stock market. I suppose this is the triumph of hope over experience; a desire to believe that some people have a quick way in making money with stocks.

The viewers comment on the videos and share the excitement of the presenter. It's like they're all gambling on the same horses at the racetrack. The thing they don't realize is that their behavior is causing the price to go up, and when shit gets real these stocks will crater fast too.

Why do people gamble on stocks? It's like believing you'll find buried treasure; as human beings, deep down we know we can't get rich quickly, but we still make risky bets that leave us broke; it's the triumph of hope over experience. I think what keeps the stock gambling alive is the occasional dopamine rush that happens when a stock goes up a lot quickly. It's like hitting the slots at Vegas; you forget those 50 handle pulls that gave you nothing and focus on that bunch of quarters sliding down the chute.

These YouTube channels claim to be showing you how to invest for the long term, but they're all hype and no substance.

When these YouTubers or people on the recently super-popular subreddit "Wall Street Bets[2]" make big mistakes they celebrate their losses by exclaiming "I just blew up my trading account." They make losing money sound cool. There's a cavalier attitude where losing money through stupid bets is a good thing. The idea of getting rich through short-term stock gambling will thrive as long as stock prices go up. I like this definition of a bull market: A random market movement causing an investor to mistake himself for a financial genius.[3]

What bothers me is that it's all like ice cream and cotton candy. It tastes good, sure, but it doesn't stick to your bones. Investments that don't grow in value aren't gains, and they should not be considered investments, they should be called gambles. People who like jumping in and out of markets should just go to Vegas where their quick wins can quickly be eclipsed by losses.

This book teaches The TITANIUM Technique, and it is exclusively for you; you won't find this anywhere else.

Each chapter emphasizes a crucial investing factor — master all eight and you'll become an expert.

The TITANIUM Technique

1. **T** - Temperament
2. **I** - Identify
3. **T** - Talent
4. **A** - A Sensible Price
5. **N** - No
6. **I** - Invest
7. **U** - Understanding
8. **M** – Moat

ONE

TEMPERAMENT

INVESTING DOESN'T REQUIRE an abundant amount of intelligence. The most important quality an investor can have is a good temperament.

The best investing habits are businesslike. You want to invest based on rational thought, not emotion. Don't get too worked up about your investments. If you become too excited or depressed about your stocks, then you're doing something wrong.

Investing is something you need to do on a regular basis, like brushing your teeth, and both produce good long-term benefits. Just as you wouldn't cry over the fact that you bought Colgate over Aquafresh when brushing your teeth, you shouldn't get overly emotional about your investments either. If you do investing right, you'll find that it's kind of boring.

"Parisian Woman at Her Toilet, 1899," You should invest consistently and unemotionally. When done properly, brushing your teeth and investing produce good long-term benefits. From Die Pariserin bei ihrer Toilette / Photo Credit: Wikimedia commons

I started investing when I was in my 20s. Back then, I simply wrote a check for $100 and put it in a stamped envelope to buy mutual fund shares. I did this every month. Invest. Rinse. Repeat. Over the years, these hundreds grew into thousands. Nothing too exciting: just writing a check, licking a stamp, sending it off. Investing is all about temperament.

And don't just take my word for it. Warren Buffett once said:

> "Investing is not a game where the guy with the 160 IQ beats the guy with the 130 IQ. Once you have ordinary intelligence, what you need is the temperament to control the urges that get other people into trouble in investing."

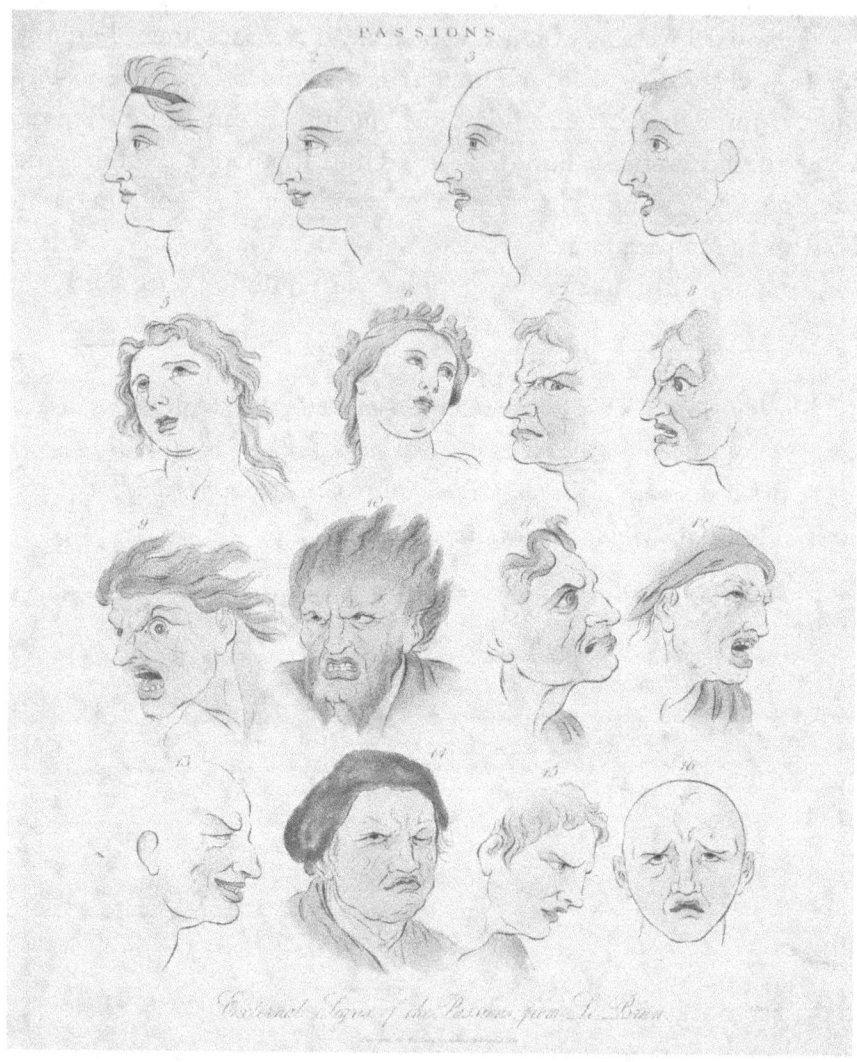

Sixteen faces depicting human emotion. The word "emotion" dates back to 1579, when it was adapted from the French word émouvoir, which means "to stir up." Engraving by J. Pass 1821 from Wikipedia.

Remember the importance of remaining calm in a storm. Be the calm sailor, eyes fixed on the horizon, guiding the boat with equanimity. Emotions are useful in many parts of our lives, but they will only prove to be a disaster for an investor.

If you get nervous seeing the stock market go up and down, you might not be cut out for investing, and acknowledging that simple fact can keep you away from bad experiences. Not everyone needs to be an investor, and knowing whether or not it makes you unhappy or uneasy is a good thing to learn in advance.

If you do invest, remember that, above all else, temperament matters. Do not get overly excited by your successes (celebrate them, but in a "proud that this happened" kind of way). Do not get too down on yourself when you make mistakes, we all do. Just learn what you did wrong and don't repeat it. Personally, I like to rub my nose in my mistakes just to make sure I don't repeat them.

A Russian proverb

"Dwell on the past and you'll lose an eye; forget the past and you'll lose both eyes."

In other words, don't dwell on your mistakes, but don't forget them either.

With each mistake you make, pick failure's pocket and learn something along the way.

Try to be Consistently Not Stupid

Charlie Munger, who has been Warren Buffett's partner at Berkshire Hathaway for decades, put it best:

"It is remarkable how much long-term advantage people like us have gotten by trying to be consistently not stupid, instead of trying to be very intelligent."

. . .

Five Stupid Decisions I Almost Made

The five stupid decisions I almost made resulted from me getting excited during two occasions when others were getting euphoric. I could have lost a lot of money in any or all of my investments. Fortunately, I did not buy any of them. But boy did I come close. Learn from my close calls. When you're getting excited about a stock or a fund, check your emotions.

1. My first mistake I could have made was that I almost invested in the Janus Twenty Fund. The fund delivered breathtaking returns to investors, more than 100% a year. It was the "Hot Fund" of its time, and investors poured billions of dollars into it (which caused its holding to go up in value, perpetuating the cycle). The 20 stocks that comprised the fund were mostly tech and Internet stocks. That fund, along with the many other tech-heavy Janus funds, lost a huge amount of money in the 2000 tech crash. It was shut down.
2. Next, I almost invested in Washington Mutual, which many believed to be an amazing bank. So many investors, even star mutual fund managers like Bill Nygren, got suckered into buying shares. True believers, like Nygren, bought large stakes in WAMU, which promptly went bankrupt during the financial crisis in 2008, and its decaying carcass was bought by Wachovia Bank.
3. I almost bought stock in California-based Golden West Financial. This mortgage lending bank was a darling to several fund investors, such as Jim Gipson at Clipper Fund. It was the stock that went up and up and up year after year, and made many investors very rich right up until the point they became very poor. Golden West invested heavily in subprime mortgages in the run-up to the financial crisis.

4. I almost bought shares of the White Oak Growth Stock Fund, a technology-heavy fund that was perpetually on the top of the hot mutual fund charts for amazing returns. I even wrote a letter (the old fashioned kind on paper) to the fund manager when I was thinking of investing. He made a small typo when describing his fund's strategy in his response to my letter. His carelessness made me think he might be overlooking important details in the fund, which eventually crashed and burned when the tech industry did in 2000. Any investors who did not flee had to wait 18 years to recover the money lost when the tech bubble burst.
5. Finally, I didn't sell during the dot-com crash. I didn't sell after the financial crisis. Just staying calm and weathering the storm prevented the permanent loss of capital.

This is but a small list of mistakes I could have made but didn't simply by not being stupid instead of trying to be very intelligent.

How I Avoided the Mistake of Investing in Stocks that Tanked

How did I not make the mistake of investing in stocks that tanked? My greed did not exceed my need to get rich off them.

Warren Buffett once said, "Rational people don't risk what they have and need for what they don't have and don't need." Though I had not read that quote at the time, I must have understood its lesson in my very bones.

I remember chatting with a woman I met at a Starbucks on 15th Ave in Seattle. I think I was reading the Business & Investing section of the Wall Street Journal and she must have said something to me about stocks. It was the late 90s and tech stocks were a hot topic, many of them gaining 50% to 100% a year. She told me about a stock called Cisco and said she had invested in it recently. I asked her what that was, but it didn't seem like she really knew anything about it. She merely explained to me that it was the stock to buy; everybody was making a ton of money on it.

I felt a twinge of regret that I was missing out on Cisco. Everyone knew about some magical tech stock and here I was without a clue as to what it was.

Yet the fear of missing out on Cisco never trumped my feeling that I didn't understand the company.

Cisco stock shot up like a rocket during the Internet craze, but its ascent was not infinite. In 2000, Cisco stock crashed like Icarus, and I couldn't be more relieved that I never invested in that stock.

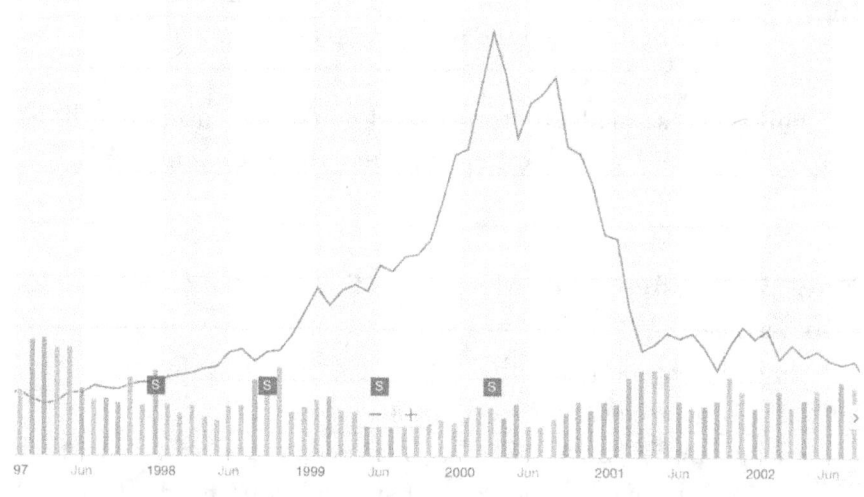

Chart of Cisco stock from 1997 through 2002. Investors who bought Cisco near its peak never broke even. Market participants get greedy and buy hot stocks at the same time. Someone told me that all her friends were buying this stock and making a lot of money. I'm glad I didn't listen. Chart from Yahoo Finance.

Look, I feel the same emotions as you and everyone else who has ever thought of buying an exciting stock. One thing that has served me well is not acting when I don't understand something.

Keep calm and focused no matter what. Remember that emotions are your worst enemy as an investor. Don't give in to the fear of missing out on the next hot stock. And certainly don't let blind greed dictate your next moves. Try to always act rationally; investing is best when it's businesslike. Follow that one simple rule and you'll do just fine.

TWO

IDENTIFY

I DECIDED TO DIG A HOLE. And not the fun kind of digging that a dog does for play. It was instead a mission to find a crack in the very foundation of my house. It was my first home and I live in rain-soaked Seattle, so after the heavy April rains saturated the dirt, they then traveled down the path of least resistance through a crack somewhere in my foundation. Next, the merciless rain slid through the concrete walls, crawling across the basement floor in dark meandering fingers that saturated the carpet. My goal was to find the crack and patch it to stop my basement from becoming a floodplain.

Some people would hire experts to do the digging and find the source of the leak. Sane people would do that. People who have full-time jobs and no time to figure out home repair would do that. But my unique blend of curiosity and crazy made me dig up my yard to find my own little private treasure; the reward for all my hard work in the hot sun would be a crack, a hole, any clue to point me toward the source of the infiltration in to my once-dry home.

Dinosaur eggs

At the bottom of the hole, my shovel struck what seemed like a boulder. I tried to lift it out with the shovel, but it was too big. I tried to get an edge of the shovel under a corner and use leverage to pry it loose, but it was too heavily secured beneath the compacted earth. I decided to try and loosen all the earth around the rock, to free it from the earth's clutches, and a long while later, I got every last bit of dirt that had been hugging it in place out of the way. The rock moved and I felt like how a dentist must feel after struggling with an impacted wisdom tooth, when finally the tools and pulling and wrenching pay off with a satisfying pop.

In my case there was no tooth, but rather an amalgam of stone, brick, and cement that were likely used as backfill 70 years ago[1] when the house was built. In the foundation repair and waterproofing business, they call these hard-to-define masses that dent your shovel "dinosaur eggs".[2]

After all the digging I finally got to the crack. A long, lightning bolt crack that extended from sea level downward. I rejoiced in a moment of glee at finding the holy grail (unless you've ever had an until-now-unknown-source-of-leaking-foundation you may never know the exuberance of finally finding the root cause).

Then, dizzy and dehydrated, I climbed back out of the hole I had literally dug for myself.

Tired and happy, I lay on my back on the front lawn. It was a moment when I could have hallucinated, but I was indeed awake and very lucid. I saw a hawk flying slow circles high in the sky, gliding on the currents of the warm June air. It was circling with intent, searching for a nutritious meal.

Identify

The hawk could find many things to eat, I'm sure. Hawks and owls typically prey on ground-dwelling mammals like mice, voles, rats, squirrels, and rabbit.

This circling hawk, though, was not looking for just any old morsel to eat. It was looking for just the right kind of small mammal, an evolutionary preference that has enabled it to survive for millions of years. As I recall from biology class, birds and dinosaurs both evolved during the Jurassic period, and their instincts are responsible for their survival, even during the Jurassic period that wiped out the dinosaurs.

The hawk was clearly looking to identify a certain, highly specific small mammal. It didn't need to get distracted by attacking another bird — falcons and owls prey upon other birds, but hawks eat mammals[3]. This hawk was taking its time to find the right opportunity.

This ability to identify a high-quality target must be the goal of the clever investor. One must possess patience and persistence, and the ability to search for exactly what you need and not settle for less. The pigeons of the world may eat just about anything thrown in front of their hungry eyes, but the hawk takes time to identify his next meal. As an investor, your job is to find what best suits you.

The qualities of the hawk are mirrored by the successful investor. Charlie Munger said, *"I think the record shows the advantage of a peculiar mind-set — not seeking action for its own sake, but instead combining extreme patience with extreme decisiveness."*

The hawk circling above could have settled for a pigeon or a mouse. I have read accounts of hawks scavenging roadside dear carcasses, dead cottontail rabbits or even doves shot by hunters[4]. When such opportunities present themselves to a hungry hawk, they're just too easy to pass up. My guess is that the hawks in my area are not starving because there's abundant wildlife in the area. They don't have to dine on roadside carrion. They seem to waste little energy as they float on thermal currents, using patience and keen eyesight — they have a 20/2 vision that's eight times more acute than humans with perfect vision. A hawk scans the landscape for a live animal that fits the profile of nutrient density, and at the right moment it swoops down and grabs that rabbit or salmon for a fresh meal[5].

It struck me that investing requires similar selectivity and decisiveness. You can buy any stock and get average results; the rats, squirrels, mice, the odd raccoon. Maybe you buy a stock that's roadkill. But please remember that you don't have to settle. You must be patient, and don't settle for just anything that crosses your path. Identify stocks ahead of time, even when prices seem high, and *then* when prices drop you can be decisive.

The gambling mindset in the stock market is based on taking action based on excitement, trading in and out, trying to buy low and sell high. Jumping in and out of the market rarely works.

So what you want to do is be as selective as a hawk. Think in terms of identifying one wonderful business that you understand well, and with time and practice, you can even add a second or third business.

Why you must know a business well

When you buy stock you want it to be a one-time event. You want to buy it with the goal of holding the stock for a long time and not having to think about selling it. You should not have to check on it every year and worry about it.

Excessive activity erodes your invested dollars. Think of holding stocks like using a bar of soap when washing your hands: the more you handle it the smaller it becomes. The same thing happens when you trade stocks: you lose money to ill-timed decisions, commissions and taxes. A great company will just compound in value over time if you just buy it and leave it along. Come back a few years later and your shares should be worth a lot more.

The other reason you want to know a business well is to avoid losing money. As of this writing we're in a bull market, and it seems like it's impossible to lose money in stocks; a rising tide lifts all boats. But things change quickly and many of the companies that seem exciting and interesting right now will cause investors to lose a lot of money. Growth stocks that have not yet become profitable are the ones that drop fastest in a stock market crash because everyone sells riskier stocks and goes toward solid companies that will be around for the long term.

So you really want to know a business well before you invest your money. For recent examples, I know people who bought a lot of Tesla stock in the $350 range, and there's no way to know if they will ever break even. People bought GoPro stock at $80 a few years ago and now it's selling for $3 and change. GameStop stock was selling in the $30 - $40 range a few years ago and it's also in the $3 range.

If you really understood Tesla, GoPro or GameStop you would have known that their businesses were in trouble. There was just a lot of uncertainty about their business models, and people who didn't know the companies lost a lot of money that they may never get back. There are many other examples, I'm just sharing a few recent examples.

Now if it were as easy as just buying stocks in big successful companies that have done well in the past investing would be easy and everyone could get rich. There are a lot of land mines that can explode your portfolio. Ask any investor in GE what it felt like to see their stock go from $30 to $15, losing half their money in a short time...and then have the stock go down to the $8 range where it sits as of this writing.

The stocks that did well a few years ago don't necessarily have rosy futures, so you have to bring an intensity to identifying the companies that are best positioned right now to succeed in the next decade so you don't have to keep checking them.

Seeing how many of my friends were using Amazon, and how every year the number has increased, showed me that their retail model was powerful and only gaining steam. Then I learned about Amazon Web Services (AWS) and how that segment is much more powerful than their entire retail operation — it could be its own stand-alone tech company. This example shows you how a deep understanding of the business helped me to gain the confidence to invest in Amazon. If you asked me to form an opinion about T-

Mobile, Schlumberger or Wynn Resorts I couldn't do it. But Amazon I understand, and identifying it as an outstanding company helped me invest with confidence. I think you will benefit if you can understand on a deep level the current success of a company, and what might fuel its continued success in upcoming years so you can sit back and let your money grow. If you neglect this step of understanding you may see your money shrink instead, and nobody wants that. So having the knowledge about the companies can change your behavior by increasing your selectivity, decreasing your action, and making sure you really understand a businesses before you buy its stock.

At Sunday brunch in Seattle

While at brunch one Sunday afternoon, a friend showed me her Robinhood stock positions and their percentage returns. Baidu, a Chinese Internet stock, was down. Tesla was down. She owned small positions in a bunch of stocks she knew little about. Then she showed me her holdings of companies she told me she knew better: Microsoft was up, Starbucks was up, along with Illumina. It was clear as day that on some level she knew these three wonderful businesses like the back of her hand. The first two companies are based in the Seattle area, and Illumina has a terrific reputation as being the best genome-sequencing corporation in the world.

What I could see is that the stocks she had not identified based on her understanding were all losing value. She bought them without much thought (she told me they were just small dollar amounts, and she wasn't too worried about them). In contrast, the companies that she did know well — Microsoft, Starbucks and Illumina — were doing well. I could see clearly that her two speculative stocks — Baidu and Tesla — were losing value and causing havoc in her portfolio, but her solid companies with wide moats[6] were doing well. If you're investing for the long term, those solid, profitable, wide-moat companies are just the kinds of businesses you want to own.

If I were to hazard a guess, I'd say that my friend likes taking a little money and putting it into speculative stocks; little gambles that might pay off spectacularly. There's nothing wrong with doing that, but I think she should do that with money that's in a separate account solely dedicated to making wild-ass bets. Never confuse gambling with investing in both your mind or in your accounts.

Paul Samuelson, who won the Nobel prize for economics, once said, "Investing should be more like watching paint dry or watching grass grow. If you want excitement, take $800 and go to Las Vegas."

You only need a few

You only have to identify a few wonderful businesses in your lifetime to get great investment returns. If you find three such businesses, you will do well. For now, though, we will be satisfied with finding just one at a time.

By the way, I just heard an interview with investor Charlie Munger, and he said he has only three investments. He owns stock in Berkshire Hathaway, Costco, and the rest is in an investment fund run by Li Lu[7] in China. Munger explained that you don't have to own stock in a lot of different companies if you identify great ones.

This chapter will show you why identifying businesses is so important and help you ask the questions that lead to identifying great businesses.

We will start with the process for narrowing down a large list of stocks into a smaller, more manageable one, and finally, I'll share with you some mistakes I've made because the more hard lessons you can learn from me, instead of from your own terrible experiences, the better off you will be.

1. I bought shares of a company called Leucadia National Corporation 15 years ago. It was a horrible decision, but I convinced myself at the time that I knew more than I

actually did. I overestimated the competence of the CEO and his business partner, and bought shares when they were pretty expensive — I clearly overpaid. I don't need to get into the details of Leucadia's business because it was complex, but the brilliant performance of the leaders did not persist into the future. Leucadia merged with Jefferies Financial Group, and a new CEO took over. Leucadia's outstanding past performance became a distant memory, and the stock never recovered.

The worst part of the Leucadia investment was that I sold all of my shares of the S&P 500 index fund to buy shares in this stock. So I went from a diversified portfolio of stocks into only two stocks I did not understand very well. This could have been a brilliant move if the two stocks performed phenomenally well, but my not understanding them turned this into a bad decision. I held the stocks for several years, but at the end of the day I would have been much better off just staying in the index fund or buying stock in a company I understood better.

1. The other stock I bought was White Mountains Insurance Group (WTM) and I did so largely because the CEO at the time was Jack Byrne, and he was a legend at the time – he was in charge of the turnaround at GEICO and was widely considered one of the most talented insurance executives. He passed away shortly after I became a shareholder and the company just sort of went nowhere. To make matters worse, I bought this stock with the proceeds of the S&P 500 index fund shares I sold to buy this stock along with Leucadia.

Selling my S&P 500 shares and going "all in" on two stocks I didn't understand well was a big mistake. I really just made what was essentially a "jockey bet" knowing nothing about the horse. I knew that the leaders at Leucadia had a great long-term record of growing the business, and I knew that Jack Byrne was an insurance superstar. So I was banking on them staying in charge of the companies and me enjoying their businesses growing for years to come, and my stock price ascending to the heavens.

What happened? Well, with White Mountains, after Jack Byrne passed away I noticed that when I read the annual report the company had stopped growing its book value per share[8] with the same regularity. The stock price was not going anywhere because the book value was not increasing, and as I held the stock it decreased or remained stagnant for years. What I hoped would be an outstanding insurance company turned out to be a dud.

Leucadia National's two solid leaders, Ian Cumming and Joseph Steinberg, decided to merge the company with Jefferies LLC, a mid-sized Wall Street brokerage firm. Jefferies' CEO, Richard Handler, became the CEO of the combined entity, which retained the Leucadia name. Shortly after the merger, Handler became one of the highest paid CEOs on Wall Street, but shareholders of Leucadia did not make out financially nearly as well as Handler. The new Leucadia languished for several years, a hodgepodge of businesses from iron ore mining in Australia, a slaughterhouse in Kansas City, and a Wall Street investment bank. It was a perfect case of what investor Peter Lynch calls "deworsification." Eventually the company was renamed Jefferies Financial Group, and ever since the entity has continued to step in one pile of manure after another, most recently a $146 million charge for an investment in WeWork[9]. Fortunately, I sold my shares of Leucadia many years ago, and the big lesson I learned is not to hold stock in a company if there's a change in leadership, because the jockey who's been riding the horse in all those winning races is now long gone!

All of these mistakes, and you're still reading a book by an author who has made such terrible decisions? Well, I promise you I have learned a few lessons from these two bad stock decisions. Please learn these vicariously, and you can save yourself thousands of dollars and the frustration of hoping for many years that mediocre companies will turn themselves around. Here is the short list of observations and lessons learned. You can learn from them and without the pain!

1. Just because a company has done well in the past, it doesn't mean this performance will continue indefinitely.
2. The talented CEO running the show may not stay there forever. They could get a better job offer and leave, retire, or some other unpredictable force could take effect. A great leader is not enough, because they may be replaced with someone worse, and you'll be left with the business. So make sure the business is bullet-proof and capable of being run by an early primate, because one day it probably will be.
3. If the leader who amassed the great record decides to leave, sell the stock! I wish I had left as soon as the leaders in charge when I bought the stock left the companies. I could have avoided so much frustration.
4. Leucadia was involved in buying distressed companies, nursing them back to health, and selling them at a high price. White Mountains Insurance sold insurance and reinsurance. I assure you, I was not an expert in either business, and I attribute my failure to the fact that I didn't thoroughly understand what I was getting into. I invested in two stocks I hoped would do well. I should have been thinking about businesses I understood instead. I'm in Seattle…Amazon, Microsoft, Starbucks anyone? Right….beneath…my nose. Don't buy stocks of companies you don't understand like I did. Go for the low hanging fruit!
5. I got lucky because despite my missteps I broke even. I held White Mountains for about three years and Leucadia for 10 years. So I didn't lose money, but if I had left the money in the S&P 500 during that time I would

have gained a lot. Fortunately I kept money in mutual funds and made a few good decisions during this time, so I kept the compounding machine running despite my best attempts to run the whole operation off the rails!

Those are my two big mistakes and the take-away lessons. I will point out that during this "decade horribilis[10]" I also made a few not-so-stupid decisions. I bought some shares of Berkshire Hathaway and never sold them. I bought shares of Carmax and Waters and never sold them. These were all companies that I understood well based on reading a ton about them. So when I talk with you about buying companies you understand, I want to help you avoid making your own horrible mistakes and just sticking to stocks in a few businesses you know well, like my Berkshire, Carmax and Waters investments. In the past several years I've only bought one new stock, and that was Amazon.

One wonderful business is all you need to get started. If you try to understand too many businesses at once, you'll get overwhelmed. Just keep it simple for now and keep your mind focused on finding one company you understand well.

Identify — You don't need to diversify

You have likely heard the advice before in articles, podcasts, and from financial media and advisers that you should diversify your portfolio. The source of much investment "advice" is people who have something to sell you — your fees are their salary. Most investors believe the mantra of mutual fund companies and financial advisors: diversify, diversify, diversify! That's great advice for about 98%-99% percent of investors out there who don't want to spend the time and energy researching businesses and valuing stocks. For those people who decide that they are happy to own part of the stock market that is a perfectly acceptable approach, and anyone can do that.

Going against the grain, however, means you have to bring added intensity to the game of finding a few great stocks. I'm a firm believer that you only have to identify a few outstanding businesses in your lifetime to build an outstanding long-term record. If the historical average returns for stock market returns are about 10% a year, then you're doing great if you can get returns of 12% to 15% or more. This seemingly small difference in percentages turns into huge differences in total returns due to the effects of that magical phenomenon known as compound interest.

Diversification is insane for smart investors

Diversification makes little sense for smart investors. If you own a diversified collection of 30, 40, 50, or 500 stocks you can't beat the market because you own so many different companies that *you are the market.* You're admitting you don't know how to analyze stocks, so you just buy a little bit of everything. You can't possibly have a firm understanding of that many companies. This approach is acceptable for people who don't understand investing and don't want to learn, but it makes no sense for those who understand investing well.

This is uncommon sense, considered absolutely ludicrous by investment advisors. They will say it's irresponsible, risky, and will probably spout off lots of reasons why you must have a diversified portfolio, the creation of which justifies their existence (via fees).

At the 1996 Berkshire Hathaway Annual Meeting[11] Warren Buffett said, "We think diversification, as practiced generally, makes very little sense for anyone that knows what they're doing." He continued:

"Diversification is a protection against ignorance. If you wanna make sure that nothing bad happens to you relative to the market you own everything. There's nothing wrong with that, that's a perfectly sound approach for somebody who does not feel they know how to analyze businesses. If you know how to analyze businesses, and value businesses, it's crazy to own 50 stocks, or 40 stocks, or 30 stocks, because there aren't that many wonderful businesses that are under-

standable to a single human being, in all likelihood. And to have some super-wonderful business, and then put money in #30 or #35 in your list of attractiveness and forego putting more money into #1 just strikes Charlie and me as madness.

"And it's conventional practice, and if all you have to achieve is average, it may preserve your job, but it's a confession, in our view, that you don't really understand the businesses that you own.

"Three wonderful businesses is more than you need in this life to do very well. The average person isn't going to run into that. If you look at how the fortunes were built in this country, they weren't built out of a portfolio of 50 companies, they were built by someone who identified with a wonderful business."

Take note of that word "identify" because it's the heart of this chapter. Your job is to be highly selective and identify one business. With time you can add more, but you really just need to start with just one.

Just to give you an idea of how I view this process, I start from a larger group of companies where I have some rudimentary knowledge of their products or services. From there, the ones that I truly admire jump out at me. I'll give you an example of 10 stocks[12] that represent my current list of great businesses, and then I'll show you the three that have jumped out at me. I'm showing you this list because I've identified these as excellent businesses for investment based on my understanding. I want to help you by sharing examples so you can see my process, but keep in mind that these are businesses I understand, and you should not buy a stock because it interests me or I own the stock. You should only buy stock that you understand well and because the business makes sense to you. I will typically spend a lot of time thinking about each of these companies before I buy the stock.

I find it helpful to write down the list on paper. You can also create a watch list online if it helps you to have a list that is regularly updated with stock prices, although I don't think it's necessary to see daily updates. Here's a list of a few companies I understand reasonably well.[13]

3M
Adobe
Amazon
Berkshire Hathaway
Carmax
Charles Schwab Corp
Costco
Intuitive Surgical
Starbucks
Waters Corp

Your list will likely be much different than mine. Because of my background, I know something about each of these companies above. You may not have heard of some of them, or might never have been a customer.

I suggest that you start by identifying a small group of companies, and you can narrow that down to those you know really well. The list above will change over time as I continue to learn about new companies, or if some of the companies change and I no longer find them worthy of consideration.

You'll probably notice that companies like Apple, Facebook, and Google are not on my list, and there are a number of reasons for that. First, I don't understand them well enough. I don't know if they will truly be resistant to competition. Second, I don't have enough confidence in their leadership. Your understanding of these companies may be different than mine, so your list may include these, but for now, they're off *my* list.

I'd like to share a few reasons why some of these companies are on my list. I'll explain why I like Adobe, Carmax and Waters[14].

1. I use Adobe Photoshop and Lightroom almost everyday in my work. I absolutely must have these apps in my workflow

and I know every other serious and amateur photographer uses at least on Adobe app. I use Lightroom to make adjustment to all photos in my collection. I use Photoshop for fine-tuning, making touch-ups, and cropping photos. I've even used InDesign to layout a book of my photography. These are all excellent apps. I have heard great things about video editing using Adobe Premiere, but I haven't yet tried it.

2. I bought my current car from Carmax, and they have a business that I think will continue to grow and succeed in the future. They make buying a used car simple because they set a price for the car that's "haggle free." I like not having to try to negotiate with the car dealer to come down from a ridiculously inflated price to a fair price. Also, Carmax pays the sales associate the same commission if they sell you a Jaguar as a Toyota, so they're not trying to upsell you on a specific car. I think it's a great business and they're expanding to have locations in many markets in the United States. I bought this stock about eight years ago and it has compounded as the company grows.

3. I came across Waters Corporation while I was searching for companies with moats about eight years ago. Waters makes scientific tools used in technical analysis for drug research, food and water safety and academic research. Their main business is selling liquid chromatography and mass spectrometry equipment — these are tools for separating and measuring very small amounts of stuff where details matter like drug development when trying to assure something is pure, and consumables for this equipment. Waters is like the Apple Computer of scientific measurement devices; they make high quality equipment and software, and the scientists I've talked with drool over these high end machines. I bought Waters stock years ago and never looked back; it's been

an outstanding investment.

I share these examples because I want you to see how a company makes my list. The three companies above I understand as a customer or observer, and I've read a lot about them, read their annual reports, and know as much as possible about each business before buying. I will remove companies if business dynamics change, and I will add new companies if I find better opportunities.

Once you've made your list, your job is to identify the one, two, or maybe even three companies that you'll buy and hold for a long time. There are many stocks that you should avoid because you don't have the competency to deal with them.

From the list above, I own these stocks:

Amazon

Berkshire Hathaway

Carmax

Waters Corp

...and I'm thinking of buying stock in Adobe, but at the moment it seems a bit too expensive to me. As you'll find in a later chapter, when possible I like to buy stock at a sensible price, and right now Adobe seems a little expensive. I will wait to see if the market declines or if it goes on sale for some other reason.

Mistakes in identifying stocks

A big mistake many investors make is to buy stocks without knowing much about the underlying companies. Your time spent identifying excellent companies will pay off for years to come because you won't have to worry about your stocks.

Another mistake people make is buying a stock because a friend tells them about it. A couple of years ago, a friend told me she invested in a tech stock called IMPINJ, which was based in Seattle. She barely knew anything about the company when I asked her what they did. The stock tanked 50% a few months later. To this day, I'm still happy I never bought the stock based on hearing about it from her.

Another common mistake people make is believing what they read in the news. Another friend of mine bought stock in TEVA pharmaceuticals because he heard Warren Buffett bought the stock. He just sped right through that mental shortcut and decided that it was a good investment. He didn't realize that the media often reports on Buffett buying a stock when in fact his holding company buying it — and someone else might have made the purchase. TEVA has been an absolute disaster since he bought the stock, with the stock declining in value continually the moment he bought it. I think he got sick and tired of the losses and just sold it for pennies on the dollar.

One of the best things to look at when identifying a new business is the talent and integrity of the company's leadership. When you have a really talented person in charge and you trust their judgment and integrity, it's a lot easier to hold the stock with confidence.

THREE

TALENT

YOUR MOST IMPORTANT JOB, once you've identified a great business of course, is to confirm that the CEO has talent.

Talent is one of the intangible aspects of investing. It's not something you can look up on a chart or calculate with numbers. You will be at an enormous advantage if you read articles and annual reports, watch YouTube videos, and listen to podcasts to discover if the CEO has talent. Here is where your critical thinking skills will shine.

I remember reading Warren Buffett's letter to Berkshire Hathaway shareholders when I was just starting out. It was written in such a simple and direct way, I was surprised that I didn't have to be a financial genius to understand it.

Buffett aims to make the letter as accessible as it is informative, and he's careful not to include too much jargon. To keep it readable, he writes the letter as if he's talking to his two sisters.

"It's 'Dear Doris and Bertie' at the start and then I take that off at the end,"[1] Buffett explained. "That's because for Doris and Bertie, Berkshire is pretty much their whole investment." And although they're both very smart, Buffett said, his sisters are not active in the business world, they're not reading about it every day. "I pretend that they've been away for a year and I'm reporting to them on their investment."

I encourage you to find out as much as you can about a given company's CEO in order to assess their talent and integrity. Pretend you're a tough-but-fair investigative reporter and you're researching for a story about them. There is an abundance of information out there in the form of articles, interviews, and videos for you to absorb. Read as much as you can, and take as much time as you need in order to figure out whether the CEO has talent. Can you trust them with your money?

Make a short list of talented CEOs based on your research. Then cross out the name of any CEO who doesn't strike you as having a lot of talent. If this person seems really smart, but there's something about them that puts you off, just go with your gut feeling and cross their name off the list. Talent is great, but if the CEO lacks integrity you're going to suffer later.

Three traits of talented leaders

A talented leader cannot see any further into the future than anyone else, they don't have a magic crystal ball telling them what happens next. What they do have, however, is the ability to predict with great accuracy what will be in demand in next five years. Talented leaders have:

1. *A customer obsession:* Jeff Bezos has a vision of customer obsession that drives the culture in Amazon's retail business and Amazon Web Services (AWS). Products fast and at low cost.
2. *A vision for the future:* BYD[2] founder Wang Chuanfu works toward clean air and pollution reduction in China and around the world with electric cars and the SkyRail monorail system.
3. *Inventing for others:* Steve Jobs invented the iPhone not

because customers asked for it, but because he anticipated their needs.

Talented leaders often started the company
Talented leaders often founded the very company they work in. They have a strong motivation to make the company a success and ensure that its culture endures long into the future. They are often the largest owners of the company's stock, and their decisions affect them just as they affect you (though they own more shares). Making money is merely a byproduct of realizing their dreams; it's seldom the motivating factor.

Eight talented leaders
There are many talented leaders in the corporate world today, and here are the eight I admire for their leadership.

1. Jeff Bezos at Amazon
2. Warren Buffett at Berkshire Hathaway
3. Pony Ma Huateng at Tencent
4. Steve Jobs at Apple
5. Satya Nadella at Microsoft
6. Steve Wozniak at Apple
7. Eric Yuan at Zoom Video

When you think of talented leaders, some other people may come to mind. You may even know some leaders with talent that few others are aware of. Keep it to yourself! This knowledge can give you a head start as an investor.

You'll notice I included Steve Wozniak along with Steve Jobs, even though he wasn't necessarily the one with the vision of what Apple would become. I include him because I want to make sure he continues to receive his share of credit for helping make Apple the powerhouse it is today.

I recently watched a refreshing interview with Wozniak on YouTube. What sets him apart from many is his total disregard for stock price, company success, or money. He is not fixated on his net worth, but only on his desire to bring great computers into the world.

The interviewer asked Wozniak how closely he watches the Apple stock price. Wozniak replied, "I do not watch it at all. Period. I've never used Apple Stock App once. I don't want to live that life of day trading, always being concerned 'this is up, this is down' because I have a philosophy of happiness, which is smiles versus frowns. You're always frowning if you're always worrying about how something's going to turn out, be it stocks, or elections, or companies progress."

He went on to say that "I never did anything for the value of the stock, and the value of the company, and the value of money... I did it to create great computers for the world."

That statement perfectly captures the mindset of a talented leader. This is not typical of leaders and CEOs in corporate America today, and part of your job is to eliminate those who do not take this approach. In my view, many CEOs and boards of directors have this dual mission: they want to grow the company, and also become rich because their jobs are not guaranteed. Unfortunately for shareholders, the money and stock options that CEOs receive are an expense that all shareholders pay. When you realize that many compensation decisions are generous grants of money from the company to the CEO you will have a new tool to use in making stock decisions.

If you are aware of the potential for overly generous compensation packages, then you can use this awareness as a powerful tool in evaluating companies. Amazon's Jeff Bezos made less than $2 million in 2018, and during the same year Berkshire Hathaway's Warren Buffett earned less than $ 0.5 million, while Disney's Bob Iger earned $65.6 million during the same year — 30x more than Bezos and 130x more than Bezos. Was Iger worth that much more to his company than Bezos and Buffett were to theirs?

I can't claim to know who deserves what in corporate life, but here is one truth I have found to be consistent across all companies: those companies that are not wasteful of shareholder money tend to spend wisely in good times and don't waste money in downturns. They are consistently responsible with the company's money. If you can find companies like this that treat shareholders like partners instead of pansies you can just buy the stock and forget about it. You can trust the CEO "eats the same cooking" as you because their primary wealth comes from their shares going up in value – not in them giving themselves huge cash payouts that come at your expense.

I once owned shares of Eli Lilly, a pharmaceutical company that developed a lot of blockbuster drugs for a string of years in the 1990s, Lipitor for cholesterol being one of the most famous. As a photographer, I admired the glossy color photos in the company's annual report; they were beautiful, and the layout was professionally designed. The annual report was printed on high quality coated paper. I know a bit about the costs for producing an annual report, and the graphic design and photography budgets are often quite large. What happened was that when the stock market crashed the company drastically cut back on their budget for the annual report. All of the sudden the budget for photos disappeared and the annual report was printed on cheap newsprint, and there were no photos – at all.

The company clearly signaled that they were cutting back on spending, and what better way to show shareholders the new approach to saving money than cutting back on the main publication sent out to all shareholders.

The problem is that the CEO, Sydney Taurel, was drawing a huge paycheck during these tough times for the company. On the one hand the main shareholder communication was greatly affected, but Taurel was still getting paid many millions a year despite the companies problems, which included laying off many employees.

Outstanding companies like Amazon and Berkshire Hathaway don't waste a lot of money on things that don't benefit customers and shareholders. Both print a "plain vanilla" annual report that's mostly devoid of photos, and they don't change things up and start saving money just because the market crashes or the economy collapses. They are consistently careful stewards of capital in good times and bad. Search out CEOs like that.

Many corporations hire compensation committees to determine how much the CEO and other executives get paid. If they do a good job (award high pay packages) then they get hired again next year. The conflict of interest in this arrangement is insane, yet it is common practice in most companies.

Therefore, much of your job is easy and requires eliminating CEOs of companies who lack talent and whose primary interest is to extract money for themselves at the expense of the business. The CEO position is often filled by people who talk a good game, can deliver sound bites perfectly on CNBC, and are always good schmoozers. CEOs are often the figureheads of a company, and they make media appearances and are good at talking in such a way as to make people like the company and feel good about its prospects. Many CEOs are good parasites — they don't kill the host, but survive off it long enough to ensure that their families and children are financially set for life before they get fired or move on.

If this seems highly skeptical or critical of the people who fill the top job in many companies in corporate America, it is. Dedication, humility and reliability take a back seat to "star quality." My personal experience is that the companies where the CEO is not paid an exorbitant salary seem to perform better. My guess is that these companies don't attract the greedy leaders.

I felt kind of alone in this sentiment, but then I read what Charlie Munger said about the greed in American business.

> *"People should take way less than they're worth when they are favored by life... I would argue that when you rise high enough in American business, you've got a moral duty to be underpaid — not to get all that you can, but to actually be underpaid."*

I'm not saying that CEOs should not be paid well, I'm just saying that the brightest and most effective leaders I observe don't reach for the last dollar.

The optimal CEO — A talented founder

The optimal situation is to buy stock in a business run by a talented CEO who is also the founder. It's best if they own a lot of stock themselves, pay themselves a small salary relative to their overall compensation (stock compensation is fine), and that they have a clear vision for what their company can become manifested by a strong company culture. Bezos, Buffett, and Jobs were mentioned earlier, and there are several other talented founding CEOs you can find with a little work.

Just because you buy stock in a company that has a talented CEO does not guarantee you will succeed in your investment. The following list will help you categorize CEOs as you learn more about them. There are three types of CEOs, and we'll look at each of them.

The talented, non-founding CEO

Some businesses depend on a talented leader, and this is especially true with tech companies like Microsoft. The company thrived under its founder, Bill Gates, but the company floundered miserably under his replacement, Steve Ballmer. There were several mistakes and lack of direction under Ballmer's leadership, and Microsoft lost its luster in almost every regard under his poor leadership. The Windows phone was never a serious competitor to the iPhone. Microsoft opened up retail locations that looked like copies of Apple Stores and in doing so almost outright admitted that they could not come up with their own original ideas.

During Ballmer's dim tenure, Microsoft developed a copycat

voice assistant called "Cortana," seemingly released as a knee-jerk reaction to Apple's Siri. I have never heard anyone (who wasn't a Microsoft employee) speak positively about Cortana. I can't say whether it's a good voice assistant or not, only that it has not been widely adopted.

Luckily, in 2014, Satya Nadella took over as CEO of Microsoft and gave focus to a directionless company.

Ever since Nadella took over as CEO, Microsoft has experienced a renaissance. Microsoft was a big, but stagnate company, and the introduction of a talented CEO made a huge difference in renewing its reputation as a global leader in tech.

Nadella has led major projects that included the company's move to cloud computing and the development of one of the largest cloud infrastructures in the world. Microsoft seems to be making significant progress with its Azure Cloud infrastructure, which has made the company competitive again. Microsoft is proof that companies need talented CEOs to succeed. Without this crucial ingredient the company flounders; with one, it can be reborn. Apple stagnated for years during Steve Jobs' absence, and when he returned to the company they invented the iPod, the iPhone, iPad, the MacBook. You get the idea.

Another good example of a talented, non-founding CEO is Adobe's Shantanu Narayen at Adobe. He has been instrumental in ushering Adobe into the cloud computing age by providing software subscription models for Photoshop, Illustrator, Premier, and several other image-editing programs. Adobe has navigated this change gracefully, and by that I mean they have maintained their strong user base despite the change from the "upgrade" cycle of selling software to the "monthly subscription" model.

Shantanu was not the founder of Adobe, but he's done a good job of moving the company forward without screwing it up. I don't know if Adobe would have made such a smooth transition to the cloud with any CEO, but there were potential problems in convincing a large number of loyal Adobe customers who were accustomed to buying software on discs to switch to a monthly subscription model. The transition to the cloud-based subscription model has gone smoothly.

I believe that all software companies will eventually switch to cloud-based subscription models as a means of survival. I myself use Photoshop, Dropbox, Microsoft, and Squarespace and pay a monthly fee for their services. I do this regardless of the CEO because I like the product. It's hard for me to know whether Shantanu is extremely talented as a CEO, but Adobe has continued to succeed in image-editing and filmmaking software during a big transition, and the company gets credit for navigating safely through potentially choppy waters.

Adobe seems to be a successful company with great image-editing and video-editing software, but I don't know how much of Adobe's success is a result of its CEO. If I were to guess, I think the quality of Adobe's products are good enough that the CEO could be replaced and the products are dominant enough that the company would survive. For example, look at McDonald's, Coke, Disney, and Nike. You may not know who the CEO is right now, they may be talented or not, but the companies are chugging right along and probably will be for the foreseeable future, regardless of who's behind the wheel.

The brilliant & unpredictable CEO

This is the genius CEO with divine talent. They are often passionate and can be viewed by some as a loose cannon, spraying Tweets and making outlandish statements to the press. These leaders have a vision and make bold, often wild bets. They often lead dynamic companies and they get great joy in taking investors on a wild ride; a current example is Elon Musk. There is no doubting Musk's brilliance and accomplishments, but it is hard to know if he has the temperament required to run a company and make it profitable for years to come. He could run the company for the next 10 or 20 years with great success, or it could go bankrupt in that time. I am cautious of talented investors whose emotions may be erratic and could stand in the way of the company achieving consistent growth over time.

You only succeed as a long-term investor if the company is profitable, and if it returns cash to shareholders through reinvested earnings (appreciation of intrinsic value) or dividends. Tesla is not yet profitable, so my point is that you should not just invest in a company simply because it has a talented, popular CEO.

The incompetent CEO

I don't recommend investing a business run by an incompetent CEO. They may be good speakers, handle interviews with ease on CNBC, and they talk a good talk. But they are have no creative vision or talent. They fill a job description and are the public face of the company, but they are don't make decisions that add value to the company. These are the figurehead CEOs of businesses like Eli Lilly, JC Penney, McDonald's, Abercrombie & Fitch, Coke, Target, Macy's, GE, Yum Brands, or Pfizer. At best they are ineffective; at worst, in cases like Enron or Valeant, they are corrupt. In many excellent businesses the CEO doesn't have to be brilliant, they just have to avoid doing anything really stupid. Outstanding businesses have such strong brands that a CEO does not need to invent anything new, or have a vision for the future, they just need to keep the train on the track.

"I always invest in companies an idiot could run, because one day one will."

WARREN BUFFETT

It makes sense to identify these types of CEOs so you don't expect much from them. If they keep the business running smoothly, that's enough. Their talent did not create the company, and their vision isn't driving it. These CEOs fill a position and if they get fired or perform poorly (like Jeff Immelt at GE) they are simply replaced by another untalented figurehead. Businesses like GE are like large government bureaucracies; they are slow movers, not dynamic, and it takes an eternity to remove an incompetent leader.

Most CEOs are looking out for themselves. It is the rare CEO who treats shareholders how he/she would want to be treated. You will be better prepared as an investor if you just assume that most CEOs view the shareholders as patsies, not as partners. Their goal is to make their company as attractive as possible to Wall Street, so the stock price goes up and they can collect their bonuses. Assume that is the case when you hear them give rosy predictions on CNBC.

What you really want is a business run by a CEO who is concerned about the well-being of the company first, and his own pay later (or not at all). That's the advantage of investing in a company where the CEO takes a modest salary and favors compensation in stock over cash.

Look for leaders with integrity

Talent is the title of this chapter, but it could just as easily be titled "Talent & Integrity" because both are crucial in a CEO. If you can't trust the CEO to do the right thing you should never invest. If you have talent but the integrity is absent you could find yourself investing in a disaster of a company.

I just read an article in *The Water Coolest*[3] that explained that "WeWork is planning an IPO later this year, but first, the company is cleaning the skeletons out of its closet in order to ensure it doesn't fall flat on its face like Uber and Lyft[4]."

One of the problems with the company is that the CEO paid himself generously for trademarking the word "We." Not wanting that to be a problem (he will likely become a billionaire if and when

WeWork goes public) he decided to return the stock. As *The Water Coolest* explained:

"In a half-hearted attempt to appease potential investors, CEO Adam Neumann is returning $5.9M of stock issued by WeWork's parent, The We Company, which the company granted its founder for trademarking "We." Let that sink in for a second ...[5]"

Neumann and co-founder Miguel McKelvey started We Holdings LLC as an investment vehicle and initially trademarked the term "We" through the company. For their bright idea to rebrand and trademark "We" the co-founders were granted millions of dollars in stock...for a decision they helped drive.

I'm glad I read this article because it helped me to understand the integrity — or possible lack thereof — when it comes to WeWork. It seems like the CEO paid himself generously (maybe too much so) for an idea he had. When the company found itself under close scrutiny before its IPO he suddenly reversed his decision to award himself the $5.9M in stock. It called into question his integrity.

According to *The Water Coolest*, "The latest hiccup rehashes concerns that the company and its less than scrupulous founder" are not acting like good stewards of the company.

The article went on to say that the company's less-than-stellar corporate governance is nothing new, as "Red flags have already been raised related to favorable loans provided to Neumann and other execs as well as the CEO's ownership of space leased to WeWork."

The reason I point this out to you is just to show you that the CEOs and leaders of many (not all) companies are looking out for their own benefit. In Adam Neumann's case, he owns more stock of WeWork than anybody else, so he wants small and large investors to buy the stock, because he will get insanely rich sitting on all those shares he owns.

As of this writing, WeWork is free-falling because one of its big investors, SoftBank asked "The We Company" (who owns WeWork) to "shelve" the IPO. Fidelity Investments announced that it cut its stake in WeWork suggesting that the company's value was worth about $18.3B. Earlier in 2019, Will Danoff, the star manager of Fidelity's Contrafund trimmed his fund's holdings of WeWork by 553,000 shares, greatly reducing his fund's holding. As *The Water Coolest* put it, "Adam Neumann really wishes he kept that $6M for trademarking 'We' right about now[6]."

Integrity is crucial to a company's success, and if you can detect it missing you might want to pass on the stock. It's not worth getting involved with any business whose CEO lacks integrity. They'll be looking out for their best interests instead of doing what's best for the business or its shareholders.

What's integrity look like?

In stark contrast to the CEO of WeWork awarding himself $5.9M for trademarking a word, Peter Lynch, investor and author of "One Up on Wall Street[7]" wrote about visiting company headquarters to get a feel for the place. While facts and figures can be found online or through a phone call to a company's investor relations department, Lynch said he got positive vibes when he saw that "Taco Bell's headquarters was stuck behind a bowling alley. When I saw those executives operating out of that grim little bunker, I was thrilled. Obviously, they weren't wasting money on landscaping the office."

As you do your research, look for companies that don't waste money on buildings, fixtures or appliances that don't directly benefit the business. Steer clear of executives that waste money on unnecessary perks or award themselves excessive pay packages. Paying attention to these details might help you steer clear of the losing businesses and focus on the winners.

There is no fast and easy way to determine whether you can trust the CEO or not. I like to read the annual report of the company (it's free and you can download it in less than a minute from the company's website). The first section of the annual report contains the letter from the CEO and you can get an idea of their plans for the company by reading that letter. That's only the starting point, though, because you need to know much more about the CEO than you can find in a letter that has often been carefully edited by the investor relations department. Often it's little more than a puff piece and can't be taken too seriously. The exceptions to this rule, however, teach you a lot about both the CEO and the company and are well worth reading.

Search YouTube for videos with the CEO — these might be videos of past shareholder meetings, interviews with the media, talks at Google, or any number of other presentations they give. You can get a good idea of the vision, energy, and integrity of the CEO based on how they talk about the company and answer tough questions (if interviewers just lob softballs at them you may never get to hear them respond under pressure—so you should crave tough questions).

Why is integrity so important?

This gets right to the heart of this book, which is getting you into stocks you don't have to worry about and that have a chance of beating the market over the long term.

You want to beat the S&P 500 index, and many of those companies are run in bureaucratic ways, they have big committees making decisions, they make acquisitions that lose the company money — and all the while these companies are slowly losing money while their executives get paid every year. You don't want to own stock in these businesses.

So *if* you are serious about beating the market, you must eliminate these companies. We'll dive into how you can do this in chapter

5 which is all about saying "no" to investing ideas. You actually gain an advantage as an investor by focusing on a few businesses that you understand, and you don't need to understand many.

The companies run by talented leaders who have integrity are not common. So you're on a detective mission to find them. Once you find them, and their business passes filters discussed in future chapters (having a sensible price and a wide moat) then you will be looking at an outstanding business.

Look at their pay packages

Taking a look at total compensation packages is a good place to start when trying to get a handle on whether the company is being run to benefit the shareholders or the CEO. While some CEOs are extremely smart and view shareholders (people like you who buy their stock) as equals, a number of CEOs are paid so richly for their work that their compensation is out of sync with the value they provide to the company.

Whether someone is worth their salary or not is always up for debate. Corporations hire "compensation committees" to act as "neutral" parties to determine CEO pay. A serious conflict of interest exists: if the compensation committee awards a generous pay package to the CEO they will likely get hired again next year. If they don't, they lose the job, so there is an incentive to give the CEO and executive team high payment recommendations because it ensures they will get hired again. It's like your dog having final authority to give you a pay raise when they you're buying their treats.

When trying to decide if a company is run for the benefit of the shareholder, or rather to make the CEO and other executives wealthy, I think it makes sense to take a close look at what kind of pay the CEO receives and use this as a way to decide if you believe the company is using cash and stock wisely. Keep in mind that some companies award compensation in cash only, some in stock (called equity), and some in both. There is no one method that is best, but as a rule of thumb, if a CEO owns a lot of stock then their interests are better aligned with those of the shareholders.

Excessive pay packages

If you want to find out what Walt Disney CEO Bob Iger made in a given year you can Google that info: here are the specific search terms I used: "Disney CEO Bob Iger 2018." What I learned was that Disney's Bob Iger earned $65.6 million in 2018. If he worked 50 weeks that year he earned $1.3 million per week or $262,400 a day. In my mind, no CEO adds a quarter of a million dollars of value to a company per day; in my opinion he's getting rich at the expense of shareholders.

If you identify an outstanding company with an underpaid leader you may be looking at a great company run by a CEO who is leading the company, but not trying to get every last dollar possible. You want the CEO to treat shareholders like partners in the business, and if they're earning an enormous salary they're in a different stratosphere.

Reasonable pay packages

Amazon's Jeff Bezos earned $1.7 million in 2018. If he worked 50 weeks that year he earned $34,000 per week, or $6,800 per day.

Warren Buffett earned $389,000 in 2018. If he worked 50 weeks that year he earned $7,780 per week, or $1,556 per day.

As you can see from comparing pay packages, the range is enormous. Is Iger's day really worth $262,400 and Buffett's day only worth $1,556?

Or is it possible that Iger is just grossly overpaid for his work and Buffett is very modestly paid for his?

There are no clear answers here, but I would say that as an investor you need to be aware of the compensation schemes, because if the CEO is making a serious error in judgment (or the compensation committee that he's hiring is incentivized to make silly pay decisions) with regard to pay, what other problems are happening within the company that you'll never hear about on the news?

Even Mediocre CEOs Get Huge Payouts

Mathematical evidence shows that there is no link between what a CEO is paid and their company's stock performance. In other words, many high-paid CEOs don't do anything to merit their expensive paychecks. This doesn't necessarily mean that we shouldn't invest in a company that has overpaid their CEO, but if I'm choosing between two companies and I see one pays a CEO salary of $5 million a year and the other $25 million a year I would think the former is operating within a more rational culture that does not support extravagant spending.

If a company you understand is making profits and doing well overall, I would not avoid investing in the stock just because compensation seems high. My advice is to keep the CEO pay issue in mind because it's one consideration that will help you form a better picture of the company when making a decision.

I invested in one company where the CEO received pay of $25 million during a year in which the company did poorly, yet he still received not only full salary but qualified for a generous bonus. The performance bar to receive bonuses at this company was so low that he qualified during a horrible year! What I should have done when I learned this was sell the stock right away; it turns out the company's profits and share price languished for several years after. Instead I made the poor decision to ignore the excessive CEO pay and hope that things would turnaround in the future.

The problem with this situation (and it happens with many companies, not only the one I describe) is that the CEO does not suffer alongside the shareholders. They receive generous bonuses and stock option awards even if the company fails. Compare this scenario to Warren Buffett's salary at Berkshire: he earned $389,000 in 2018. He did not ask to be paid millions a year to do his job. He profits if the value his company's stock goes up. You want *that* kind of situation, where a leader experiences the same success as the shareholders because the value of their stock and yours increase or decrease in tandem.

What are these CEOs doing to justify millions of dollars per year? A study by Bloomberg Businessweek,[8] based upon data by Equilar, revealed that there was virtually no correlation between CEO pay and company performance.

In a nutshell:

1. Look to invest in a company with a talented CEO, especially if they're the founder.
2. Search out CEOs with most or all of their net worth in company stock.
3. Be wary of erratic CEOs, especially if their company is not yet profitable. You should seek to invest in a stable business for the long term.
4. Realize that some CEOs simply lack talent. Just because they got the job doesn't mean they are helping the company. Some CEOs destroy value.
5. Some wonderful businesses succeed because they have great products and systems in place where they do not require a competent CEO to function.

FOUR

A SENSIBLE PRICE

Dollar bill shirt folded and photographed by Jeff Luke

MANY PEOPLE GET SO excited to buy stock that they don't realize the price they pay has an enormous impact on their future returns.

I will tell you now that some of my best investments were total luck. I didn't know anything except that I liked the companies and stock price had little significance. I was fortunate enough to be able to invest in great businesses, such as Berkshire Hathaway, Carmax, and Waters Corporation, but that was more because of opportune timing than investment savvy on my part.

Later, I got excited about a few other companies, and again I bought in when I had the money. This time, though, I paid too much, and because my purchase price was so high, when I eventually sold many years later I had made no money on my investment. It was better than a loss, sure, but it was still a waste of time. Had I been more patient, I could have avoided this very preventable mistake.

You will find that as you invest, sometimes you will buy at a good price and sometimes you will pay too much. Your goal should be to try to be consistently patient and wait for opportunities to arise. These generally come when the stock market is cratering and everyone is scared. It's also the most difficult time emotionally to buy stocks, but it can be the most rewarding financially.

The one great piece of advice to take away here is to be patient and always have some cash on hand so you are prepared to take advantage of market crashes — which will definitely occur throughout your investing lifetime.

Charlie Munger explains why waiting is so hard:

"You have to be very patient, you have to wait until something comes along, which, at the price you're paying, is easy. That's contrary to human nature, just to sit there all day long doing nothing, waiting. It's easy for us, we have a lot of other things to do. But for an ordinary person, can you imagine just sitting for five years doing nothing? You don't feel active, you don't feel useful, so you do something stupid."

Buying stock near its all-time high is a disaster and you may never recoup your funds. I know people who bought Tesla a couple of years ago when it was at its all-time high. The excitement was so intense that everyone who loved the car (which I totally understand) got exuberant about the stock (a rookie mistake, Cotton, you hate to see it).

Everybody getting excited about a stock should be a warning to you. It can keep you out of trouble, and out of the horrible kind of value-destroying decisions that leave you with less money and more regret.

The following paragraph has the most "on target" ideas about finding "a sensible price" that I can hope to give you. As you learn and experience more about investing, remember these simple concepts:

As stock prices rise, the odds start turning against investors. When stock prices fall, the odds begin to work in your favor.

If you stay fully invested in the stock market when it rises, you won't have any cash to invest with when the market crashes.

It doesn't matter how cheaply you can buy great businesses when the market crashes, if you don't have cash on hand you're never going to make money.

If you can keep cash on the sidelines and not invest it all when the stock market rises, you'll be rewarded with fantastic long-term returns.

There is no way to know exactly what price you should pay, but if you follow the stock for a while you will likely find brief moments when a company has earnings that cause the stock to fall. Or there could even be external economic or political factors that provide you with a golden opportunity to buy stock at a sensible price. Make sure you're prepared by having a firm understanding of the company, and then do nothing but sit back, crack open a cold one, and wait. And wait.

Intrinsic Value

We know that *price is one thing*, and *intrinsic value* is another. Sometimes the price accurately reflects the value of the item purchased, and sometimes it doesn't. One thing's for sure: the price you pay has an enormous impact on future returns. Here's an example: say you want to bring home a pint of Ben & Jerry's ice cream and you go to the store. You probably already have an idea of what it will cost right now. My guess is the range is between $3 - $5.50

depending on whether it's on sale and where you buy it. Now what if you stopped by a store for ice cream and it cost $10 for that same pint? How about $20? You wouldn't buy it (I'm guessing, but maybe if you were really craving ice cream). You'd just say no and go to some other store. This is because you know, based on your extensive, life-long ice cream buying experience, that the *intrinsic value* of a pint of delicious ice cream is five bucks or less.

The same goes for donuts. You know that the *intrinsic value* of a basic donut these days is about $1 and if you go to a fancy donut cafe you might pay $2.50 or more for a donut with special toppings. But if someone tried selling you a $10 donut you wouldn't do it.

Now what's going on in the stock market *right now* is that the stock market is offering $20 pints of ice cream and $10 donuts. The *prices* of some stocks are too high and decoupled from the *intrinsic value* of the company. This makes no sense at all. In some cases (I'm talking Uber, Lyft, Tesla, Beyond Meat, and many others) these companies are selling stuff but not making a profit. In other words, they're *losing money* and have negative intrinsic value, but investors are paying inflated prices because they have dreams of a bright future. That's not investing, that's speculation. That's like paying $30 for a donut because you think you can sell it to someone else for more in the future. This party will end poorly...lots of expensive donuts and nobody to buy them. That's what stock market crashes do...they bring overpriced stock shares back to earth. It's nature's tough love way of saying "get real, stock market, you're dreaming!"

If you want better than average returns, pay attention to the price you pay and the intrinsic value of what you get in return. In this chapter we will look at ways to determine what a company is worth in its entirety, and what the price per share should be for its stock. We will then compare this to the market price of the stock to see if it's selling for a sensible price.

Let's Take a Look at Starbucks

I made a YouTube video a couple of years ago where carried out the three step process above on Starbucks, a company I understand pretty well as a Seattle resident. I made the YouTube video on August 21, 2017[1] . I just reviewed the video to find the numbers I used so I can show them to you.

1. What I would pay for the entire Starbucks corporation $80,000,000,000
2. Shares outstanding: 1,440,000,000
3. $80,000,000,000 ÷ 1,440,000,000 = $55.55 per share

The stock price for Starbucks (ticker symbol SBUX) at market close on 8/18/2017 was $52.70.

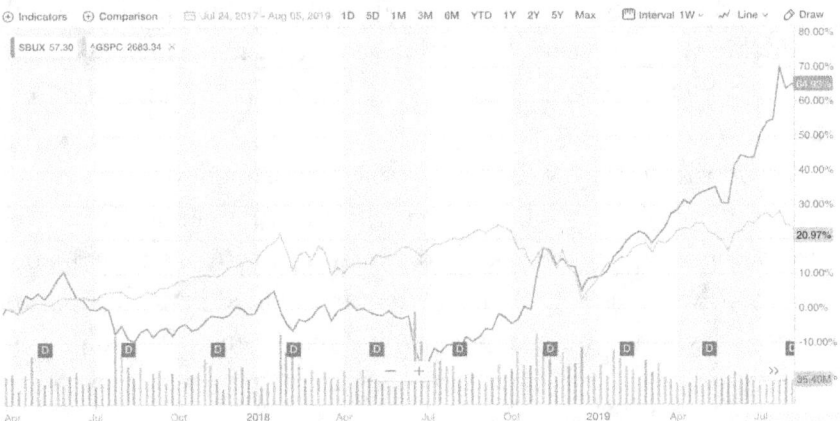

Stock Chart / Yahoo Finance

The $55.55 per share calculation of what Starbucks' business was worth was actually greater than the closing price of $52.70. In my estimation, the market was undervaluing Starbuck's stock. This is the ideal situation you want to look for: the market's quoted price is less than your estimate of the company's value.

. . .

Does Adobe sell at a sensible price?

I want to own stock in Adobe Corporation (ADBE). I understand it well, I use their products. I want to buy it already! How about the price? Is the stock currently selling at a sensible price in relation to its intrinsic value?

Let's take a look. I do all of my research and thinking and at the end of it I decide that if I were a buyer, and I decided to buy the entire Adobe business I would pay $125 billion. Now I need to know how many shares are outstanding as of September 2019, and I Google "Adobe shares outstanding" and find that in Q3 2019 there are 490 million shares outstanding.

Quick math shows that $125,000,000,000 ÷ 490,000,000 shares = $254.58/share

So I've done this quick math without looking at the stock price. Now that I've done my back-of-the-napkin calculation of what I think the stock price *should* be, I Google the actual share price, which is $277.43[2]. So the stock is only about 8.2% "overvalued" based on my math.

Obviously if I were willing to pay more money — say $137 billion instead of $125 billion, then with the same number of shares outstanding, the price per share I'd be willing to pay would work out to $279.59 which is slightly more than the quoted price. Therefore, buying today at the quoted price would make sense. It wouldn't be "cheap" and give me a large margin of safety, but it would be a fair price and a good place to start.

But in reality, I would be willing to buy shares of Adobe at about $254.58. Just to be flexible in my thinking, I don't really want to only buy it at that exact price, because I might sit around waiting forever and it would not dip to exactly that dollar figure. I don't want to be sucking my thumb and never buy Adobe because the exact price I wanted was not delivered on a silver platter.

So, I set a price range that — if the stock price reached that range — I'd be comfortable buying the stock. I'd say anywhere around $250 a share or below would definitely catch my attention. $200 would be an excellent price to begin a position in Adobe.

The challenge for any investor

The challenge for any investor is estimating what the entire business is worth. There is no shortcut for this, and no way to look up the number. If you look at the stock price or market cap you're barking up the wrong tree, because these numbers are all based on market prices of the stock — and the market can both greatly overvalue and undervalue a business.

Your job is to identify these discrepancies, and you can only do this when you decide on the truth value of the company yourself. It takes time and effort to do your own research and come to an understanding, but be patient and learn as much as you can. As you can see in the Starbucks example above, it took quite a while for the market to realize that the business was worth more. The stock was cheap for a couple of years before the market noticed it was undervalued. This presented the patient investor with an excellent opportunity.

Now you might say, looking at the graph above, that an investor would have had to wait about two years for the market to recognize the value of Starbucks stock. That's true, and sometimes it takes longer. The economist John Maynard Keynes said, "The market can stay irrational longer than you can stay solvent." In the case of Starbucks, it was a relatively short time before the stock price started to climb, but sometimes this takes a long time.

Your goal should be not to buy stocks to try to make quick money, as short-term market fluctuations are impossible to accurately predict. As Buffett said, "If you aren't willing to own a stock for 10 years, don't even think about owning it for 10 minutes."

You get rich in the waiting

Your goal should be to try to be consistently patient and wait for opportunities. These generally come when the stock market is cratering and everyone is scared. It's also the most difficult time emotionally to buy stocks, but the most rewarding times financially. Rich people get that way by not going after every opportunity, but they wait for the few times that stocks get very cheap.

The one great piece of advice is to be patient and always have some cash on hand so you are prepared to take advantage of market crashes — which will definitely occur during your investing lifetime.

Charlie Munger explains why waiting is so hard:

"You have to be very patient, you have to wait until something comes along, which, at the price you're paying, is easy. That's contrary to human nature, just to sit there all day long doing nothing, waiting. It's easy for us, we have a lot of other things to do. But for an ordinary person, can you imagine just sitting for five years doing nothing? You don't feel active, you don't feel useful, so you do something stupid."

Buying stock near its all-time high can be a disaster from which you'll never recover. I know people who bought Tesla a couple of years ago when it was at its all-time high. The excitement was so intense that everyone who loved the car (which I totally understand) got exuberant about the stock (a rookie mistake) and people who bought anywhere between $350 and $385 in 2017 may never break even. It's actually possible that the stock was overpriced based on hopes and dreams, and those who overpaid may learn the lesson not to overpay the hard way.

Everybody getting excited about a stock should be a warning to you. It can keep you out of trouble, out of the horrible kind of value-destroying decision that leaves you with less money and more regret.

This next paragraph has the most "on target" ideas about finding "a sensible price" that I can give you. As you learn and experience more about investing, I believe you will remember these simple concepts:

- As stock prices rise, the odds start turning against

investors. When stock prices fall the odds start to work in your favor.
- If you stay fully invested in the stock market when it rises, you won't have any cash to invest with when the market crashes.
- It doesn't matter how cheaply you can buy great businesses when the market crashes, if you don't have cash you're never going to make money.

If you can keep cash on the sidelines and not invest it all when the stock market rises — if you can prepare with cash to buy stocks when they're cheap you you'll be rewarded with fantastic long-term returns.

There is no way to know exactly what price you should pay, but if you follow the stock for a while you will likely find brief moments when a company has earnings that cause the stock to fall, or economic or political factors provide you with opportunities to buy stock at a sensible price. Make sure you're prepared by understanding the company, and then do nothing but wait.

The nitty gritty of finding a sensible price:
This is the secret that I seriously doubt many people use when deciding on what to pay for a stock. I share it with you because you deserve to know the best way to figure out a sensible stock price.

What I'm about to show you is simple. It doesn't take any math skills beyond those you learned in 5th grade, and you need only to search online for a couple of pieces of information and write them down, which should only take you a minute.

Once you understand this simple system you will be world-class in detecting sound prices and saying "no" to inflated prices.

Opportunity knocks

When stocks get cheap, sometimes the window of opportunity to buy is brief. I've seen stocks get cheap for a few days, and sometimes a week or two, but rarely longer than that. And this is often due to an unpredictable event; the company might have missed analyst-earning predictions, maybe the head of the Federal Reserve said something that spooked investors or perhaps a foreign country shot down a US plane.

When these kinds of events happen, a collective hysteria grips the stock market. Almost all stocks go down at the same time. Sometimes the losses are steep and sudden, sometimes they are gradual and prolonged. Whatever the cause, your friends, family, and co-workers will probably start talking about the dangers of the stock market. But these are the times when successful investing lifetimes are forged.

You must be prepared to buy the stock you've identified when the price becomes sensible, or if you're lucky, really, really cheap. All the waiting in the world is worthless if you don't have cash to deploy the moment you need it. You only have to act decisively.

You should be aware of the real possibility that stocks will drop a lot for whatever reason… and then continue to drop for weeks, months, or even years in a row. I have not experienced this happening for more than about 2-3 years at a stretch, but here are my words of caution to you: if the markets drop a lot, don't spend all of your investable money at once. Make sure to "keep some of your powder dry."

I have witnessed markets drop by 10% or 15% in a day, and that's when I happily bought some stock. A week later stocks dropped another 10%, and a month or two later another 20%. Market crashes are devious like that, they don't happen all at once, and they're often like prolonged, breathtaking plunges. And just when you think you've held on for dear life for the final drop, it falls again.

Be ready to buy at low prices

I like to have a few stocks that I'm thinking of buying on a list. I write their current price quote, and next to that the price at which I'd like to buy. I write this for a few stocks I'm considering, because if I follow five stocks there's a greater chance that one of them will decline by 10% or 20% than if I just focus on one stock. Make a "watch list" and stay focused on those stocks.

There are two ways I like stay up to date with stock prices so I'll know when a stock I'm considering drops in price. I use the app StocksTracker, and I also set alerts through my brokerage account. It's easy to do and usually found under the heading "Manage Stock Alerts."

I'll describe the StocksTracker phone app later in this book but it's free and easy to follow stocks or create watch lists to follow a group of stocks. Another thing I like about the app is that you can see price changes in real time throughout the day.

Bear in mind, one thing I don't do is trade through the app. I only make watch lists that contain the stocks I'm considering buying while I wait to see if they drop by 10% or more.

Set email alerts via your brokerage app

There are many online brokerages that let you set alerts so that if a stock you're interested in buying drops by a certain dollar amount, or by a certain percent, it sends you an email. I have used alerts in the past and they are convenient.

In reality when I'm thinking of buying a stock I'm usually following the price from day to day, so I don't need the brokerage to send me an email; I know if the price has dropped and I'm ready to buy.

However, there are times when a stock drops unexpectedly and if you're at work or not paying attention it can be helpful to have an email alert hit your inbox to let you know about the price change.

. . .

Random dude from local Starbucks

I was at Starbucks talking with this guy named Bryan who I met a while back. He's kind of a Starbucks friend, we don't hang out elsewhere, but when we cross paths there we chat about random stuff. He dabbles in stocks, and he told me that lately he's trying to make money trading biotech stocks. You may know people like him, he invests in his free time, always trying to get rich quick jumping in and out of stocks, thinking he has an edge or knows what's going on. He owns about 20 stocks, all new investments, and he'll probably trade in and out of them, pretending that he's making money but probably losing because he doesn't have a businesslike approach or reliable system.

He and I talked about stocks, and since he's a trader it's clear we take a different approach. I take a business like approach and view buying a stock as buying part ownership in that business. I don't care if the stock market is open or closed today or tomorrow because I'm owning part of a business that I hope will grow its profits and return even more cash to me in 3, 5 or 10 years then it generates today. It's a very simple concept to understand.

Just so you'll know—I only own five stocks, and one of those stocks was a spin-off, I didn't even want it, but it's sitting in my account. So I only own four stocks that personally bought, and don't have plans to sell them any time soon. That is not a diversified portfolio, but they are outstanding companies and I'd rather add more money to those unless I find something better, which I haven't found in years.

He said something that is partly true, but I think it's based on short-term thinking. He told me that whenever he looks at Amazon's stock, it's always trading at its 52-week high. Apparently that has deterred him from buying the stock — the appearance that it is always expensive. It may appear that way because the stock price has been going up for years, but upon close examination there have been times when Amazon stock has gone on sale.

I don't know how closely he looked at Amazon's stock price, but

I'm pretty sure he was giving his general feeling about Amazon being expensive, but not actually paying close attention to finding a sensible price. The graph below shows that Amazon stock declined from its highs of $2,000 and became much less expensive. Any investor who was paying attention to Amazon's stock price using the StocksTracker app or any other phone app could have seen Amazon stock fall to the $1,500 range and then $1,400. This presented the prepared investor with the opportunity to buy Amazon stock relatively cheaply.

This chart shows that Amazon stocked dropped from $2,000 a share to $1,500 and then $1,400. A prepared investor who was monitoring the stock could have bought Amazon stock cheaply. Chart / Yahoo Finance.

If you look at the chart of Amazon's stock price in 2018 you'll see that while Amazon shares climbed from April through July, the stock price declined and there were opportunities for the investor who wanted to buy shares to do so in the 1400 range (and even the high 1300s late in the year).

The casual observer who says that a stock's price "is always too expensive" might not monitor the stock closely enough. If you aren't truly focused on the company and stock price why should you expect to take advantage of a rare opportunity? The alert investor will pick that ripe fruit from the tree at an opportune time and deserves the reward. The investor who casually glances up and says "nothing's ripe" may miss something.

I believe that the prepared mind that is decisive at the right moments can take advantage of market fluctuations and buy shares at a sensible price.

. . .

A sensible price for sure?

It's always hard to know at the moment you buy stock if you are paying "a sensible price" compared to what the stock may trade at in the future.

I don't think you should be too concerned about getting a precise price, but rather try to buy stock in a range that makes sense. All you have to go on is the historical prices for a stock, and they don't tell you anything. The right question to ask is whether it's a great company, and avoid buying it at it's all-time high. I prefer to wait for a stock to pull back on negative news about the company, which is often of a temporary nature, or news affecting the economy that will affect the stock market that day, week or month but that will usually blow over with time.

You never know until years have passed if you got a great entry price into a stock or you paid too much. You can tilt the odds in your favor by taking the advice of Benjamin Graham, who was the father of value investing and teacher and mentor to Warren Buffett.

"Never buy a stock immediately after a substantial rise or sell one immediately after a substantial drop," Graham said. When you're thinking of buying a stock, ask yourself if it's selling at its all-time high. It's natural for you (or anyone) to be most excited about buying a company when its stock price keeps going up. But keep in mind it's what they call "priced to perfection," which means the stock price assumes everything will be blue skies and apple pie. Any bad news about the company or economy can take that air out of the company in an instant, and the stock price can fall fast. Don't buy stock just because everyone else is buying. Buy stock because you understand the company and it's selling at a sensible price.

Also, make sure to spread your purchases out over time. You take a lot of risk if you buy in all at once because you could be buying everything at or near a price peak. Instead, if you have money to invest, buy stock in a few different trades over at least a year, and preferably a larger time frame. This way you reduce the risk of putting all your money to work and overpaying for stock.

Don't worry, nobody "knows" ahead of time that they price they are paying is low. Many "value" investors who specialize in buying cheap stocks, or those whose value they determine to be far greater than the price they pay...only to find that the price continues to decline, sometime for years.

Nobody knows the perfect price to buy any stock. The stock price on any given day is just the consensus on that given day based on all commonly known information about a company's financial condition and future prospects.

If you think about buying a quality business and holding for a long time you will be focusing on what's truly important. Picking the perfect price will be less crucial when you look at your decision five, 10 or 20 years later.

When to buy stocks

I like to buy stocks when the market crashes. I never worry about stock prices plunging, because I plan to invest for many years and I view every price decline in a business I love as a buying opportunity.

Even if the market does not crash 30% to 50% you can still get decent bargains during occasional market declines. As Charlie Munger said, "Successful investing requires this crazy combination of gumption and patience, and then being ready to pounce when the opportunity presents itself, because in this world opportunities just don't last very long."

You will do well if you can wait until a stock you understand has declined in price by 10% to 20%. Any time I see this kind of discount in the stock of an outstanding business I get ready to pounce. I think it makes sense to write down a price range that you want to buy at, and just be patient. You will be prepared if the stock eventually declines into the price range you set. Your willingness to buy stocks should increase as their prices fall.

FIVE

NO

"*THE DIFFERENCE between successful people and really successful people is that really successful people say no to almost everything.*" — Warren Buffett

You can instantly improve your investing results if you learn to say "No" to any stock you don't understand.

Many of us try to do too many things and understand too much. It's a common mistake in our Internet culture because we're inundated with data every day, and our brains try to make sense of it all.

With investing you can just skip over the weeds and water the flowers, and this chapter will reinforce the value of saying no to every stock idea that you don't understand, and also set priorities for larger goals you'd like to accomplish in life.

Say no to multitasking

We live in the age of screens. I personally spend hours a day working on my laptop and staring at my phone — there's a good chance you do too. I wish I could say it's all time spent productively, but my YouTube history suggests otherwise. I'm constantly hypnotized, having fun, but I know I won't ever get that time back. My only solace is knowing that some of what I watch is instructive and the "recreational" time I spend looking at a screen helps me "reset" after long hours of work. But if I replaced screen time with reading more books on the printed page would I be able to think more deeply?

I like learning from people who have succeeded doing the things I admire. As a photographer, I've had the chance to make friends with, work alongside, and learn from the crème de la crème, and as an investor I absorb the wisdom from the greatest investors both alive and dead.

Charlie Munger once explained how reading is absolutely essential if you want to think deeply, and that multitasking destroys your ability to do so.

"I think people that multitask pay a huge price," he said. "They think they're being extra productive, and I think they're out of their mind," he said. Munger went on to say that the current generation spends a lot of time tuning into electronic devices and multitasking, and he thinks that when you multitask so much you don't have time to think about anything deeply.

I grew up without devices and now I use them often, so I know what learning was like before the Internet. In the early days it took hours to do the research you can do in a minute today. But then you thought more. You spent a lot of time finding books or magazines in the library, and because it was so time intensive you actually spent more time reading and thinking about a subject, and then presenting it to your class. Now we can research in seconds on our mobile devices or laptops, and we drink from a firehose of information. We are ingesting more data but we don't have as much time to think because we're distracted by the next alert, notification, direct message, Instagram post, Snapchat or text. Our collective attention span has decreased from a half hour or an hour to a minute or less.

How does this affect our thinking? Well, I think that all of the scrolling bathes us in the trivial, and all the texts, photos and video washes over us without ever sinking in. On the other hand, when you spend time to read something, or write about it, you're forced to slow down and *think*, and make connections when you think deeply.

In contrast to deep thinking about investing, there is a subreddit called Wall Street Bets[1] (WSB) which epitomizes short-term thinking. Visitors who post to WSB showcase their stock bets or share screenshots of their "all in" orders to buy enormous amounts of stock, often all in one company. The subreddit is a showcase of speculation. Frequent posters seem to bathe in the fools glory of bets gone horribly wrong. People who lose a lot of money to frivolous bets are celebrated, and a cavalier attitude toward losing money is cheered on by the rubberneckers who drive by and leave a few words of encouragement to cheer on the big bet if the gamble works out, but especially if it fails.

The subreddit is an interesting place to visit to see the outrageous bets that some people take and the amount of money they wager on stocks and options. While I find it an interesting place to visit, it seems to have attracted a loyal following of people who share a common language when talking about making bets on stocks.

What's wrong with bets?

Is there anything wrong with the "Wall Street Bets" way of thinking? Well, there are two qualities that don't accompany good investing: getting emotional, taking a cavalier attitude about investing, and they are betting seriously instead of occasionally as a pastime. This is a serious mistake because it's something done for the excitement rather than getting rich through good decisions.

The problem is that with every stock buy at a certain price, someone has decided to sell; it's the modern struggle for survival by accumulating or discarding resources instead of hunting or trading food or furs. But some people will win and some will lose, and when you pay too high a price to buy stock, or you panic and sell low, you are giving someone at the other side of the trade a better deal.

Unless you're heir to a fortune, you're giving the world an advantage and you shouldn't do that. From an evolutionary standpoint, you're going to die if you lose all your resources. Almost everybody who jumps around betting on stocks, wants to get rich quickly and multitasks on their smartphone all day is drifting into that mistake.

If you don't want to be a disaster, then read a lot and concentrate hard on something that is important. That is how you succeed. You won't succeed in life by intelligence, you'll succeed because you have a long attention span.

Gain focus by saying "no"

So paying attention to too many different things makes it impossible for us to focus and have a long attention span. But how do we make time to think deeply when there is so much we want to accomplish? The key is to concentrate on what's most important. Take a simple idea and take it seriously.

In the words of Warren Buffett, "You've gotta keep control of your time, and you can't unless you say no. You can't let people set your agenda in life." Here's a great story from the book "The Snowball: Warren Buffett and the Business of Life"[2] that I'd like to share.

Warren Buffett taught Mike Flint, his personal airplane pilot for 10 years, a special lesson on how to focus. It's a simple system, and you can easily follow along with a pen and piece of paper. To begin, you have to make a list of 25 goals you want to achieve.

Step 1: Buffett started by asking Flint to write down his top 25 career goals. So, Flint took his time and wrote them down.

Step 2: Then Buffett asked Flint to review his list and circle his top five goals. Again, Flint took some time, made his way through the list, and eventually decided on his five most important goals. (Note: If you're following along, complete these first two steps before moving on to Step 3.)

Step 3: At this point, Flint had two lists. The five items he had circled were List 1 and the 20 items he had not circled were List 2.

Flint said that he would start working on his top five goals right away. And that's when Buffett asked him about the second list. "And what about the ones you didn't circle?"

Flint replied, "Well, the top five are my primary focus, but the other 20 come in a close second. They are still important, so I'll work on those intermittently as I see fit. They are not as urgent, but I still plan to give them a dedicated effort."

To which Buffett replied, "No. You've got it wrong, Mike. Everything you didn't circle just became your avoid-at-all-cost list. No matter what, these things get no attention from you until you've succeeded with your top five."

Buffett's system increases your focus and shows you what truly matters. Items 6 through 25 on List 1 are all of the things you really want to do and are important to you, but they're second fiddle to your top five goals. Better to cut out these distractions so you can focus on what matters in your life.

Look at it this way: if you pursue all of your other priorities, you'll have 20 half-finished, half-assed projects and none of your priorities finished. Do the math on that and you'll realize there's not much there you can take to the bank.

You risk becoming a jack of all trades and a master of none. A master investor like Warren Buffett knows that to be really good at anything you must say "no" most of the time and this simple exercise is a way for you to say "no" to 20 that seem important to you but you can really do without. But to leave you with a glass half full, this does let you say "yes" to your priorities.

Stick to Your Best Ideas

Saying "no" effectively is what separates the best investors from everyone else. When they think deeply they can focus on one, two, or three companies and get to know them really well. They put their energy and time only into those. They are not foolish enough to think they can understand 30, 40, or 50 businesses.

It's "Too Hard" to know everything

You should be able to say that some investments are "too hard" to understand. There's no shame is not being an expert on every business. If you're fortunate to understand a few businesses very well you'll do better than spreading yourself thin trying to form an opinion about many companies.

If you invest in only five companies and you screw up because you don't really understand two of them you may lose a lot and your overall returns will suffer; a few big losses can destroy your account.

Example of "too hard"

I'm currently thinking of investing in a few stocks. Each company has something about it that interests me, but I'm not an expert in all of them. In fact, I would like to own them all, but I only truly understand a few of them. I want you to see my method, so I'm sharing my list with you here: I don't currently own any of these stocks[3]:

1. Apple (AAPL)
2. Booz Allen Hamilton (BAH)
3. Costco (COST)

4. CVS (CVS
5. Fortive (FTV)
6. Illumina (ILMN)
7. Intuitive Surgical (ISRG)
8. Medtronic (MDT)
9. Microsoft (MSFT)
10. Progressive (PGR)
11. Schlumberger (SLB)
12. Seattle Genetics (SGEN)
13. Starbucks (SBUX)
14. T-Mobile (TMUS)
15. T. Rowe Price (TROW)

There's something about each of these companies, based on of my research, that could make them outstanding investments. Yet I have to say "no" to most of them because right now I really only understand five of these companies: Adobe, Apple, Costco, Microsoft and Starbucks. I'd be comfortable buying and holding those four stocks for 10 years or longer.

Now that doesn't mean the others aren't great companies, and some might perform better than those I understand. But the point is that I should not think I can reasonably invest in all 14 companies and have "above average" results. I don't deserve to understand all 14 companies that well. If I understand five of them really well, then it's foolish to start putting money into my sixth best idea.

Seattle Genetics is too hard

Seattle Genetics works to improving patient outcomes with advanced antibody-drug conjugate technology. Their drugs deliver cancer-killing therapy to tumor cells. They have developed a drug called Adcetris that selectively targets tumor cells expressing the CD_{30} antigen, a defining marker of Hodgkin lymphoma. Sales of

Adcetris were $159 million in 2018, yet despite the success of this drug, the overall company is not yet profitable.

This company could be a fantastic investment, but I do not know about the pharmaceutical industry yet to be an educated investor. The information above was easily found in less than one minute with an online search. But anyone can find that information, and I have no advantage over any other investor.

So for me, I have to realize that an investment would be "too hard" for me. If I bought the stock now, I'd be hoping the price goes up, but this would not be based on understanding the company or its drug pipeline, or the likelihood that other drugs in its pipeline will be approved.

For me, I wouldn't be comfortable owning that stock for 10 years, so it doesn't qualify as an investment. It would be a gamble. There is nothing wrong with a speculative gamble, but I'm teaching you the no bullshit way of investing, and that is all about including wisdom and smarts, and part of that requires that you stick to the areas where you have an advantage, and saying NO to everything else.

Does "intelligent speculation" exist?

There are other stocks on that list, along with Seattle Genetics (SGN), that could be excellent investments for people with deeper understanding of a specific industry. Progressive (PGR) is a well-run insurance company, but I don't have any knowledge that makes me an expert on insurance companies. Illumina (ILMN) is the leader in gene sequencing, but I don't know that area of science particularly well. Medtronic (MDT) is an industry leader in medical devices, but I don't know their competitive advantages as well as a surgeon, physician's assistant or nurse who uses Medtronic's products every day.

Now even though I just told you I'm no expert in any of those companies, I do think that there is a way to "speculate" in a smart way. Yes, you heard right! I'm saying you can gamble with stocks you don't understand really well in such a way that you limit your risks.

Ben Graham[4] made a distinction between investment and speculation.

"An investment operation is one which, on thorough analysis, promises safety of principal and a satisfactory return. Operations not meeting these requirements are speculative."

If I invested in any of those 15 companies, to be honest I'd mainly just hope they went up in price. I'd be thinking, "well, I've heard of this company and I think they're probably pretty good at what they do, but I'm no expert in that field" and that's different than understanding the business well.

Yet Graham draws a line between speculation and intelligent speculation, and he says that intelligent speculation leans toward the mathematical possibilities and measurement of the odds on experience and the careful weighing of relevant facts. He's saying you can take on some risky stocks if you are thoughtful about what you're doing and try to guess the odds that things will work out.

I believe that you can invest in a few risky stocks (don't go all in, obviously) and that the ones that work out spectacularly could make up for the bets that didn't materialize. It's all about going in with a plan and realizing that it's experimental, and by definition that means you don't know the result, but that's what intelligent speculation is all about.

Graham says that you can combine intelligent speculation with diversification, and that will increase your chances for success. He says that instead of just making one big bet (speculation) you can diversify by making many small bets (intelligent speculation)[5].

"Sometimes your speculation will work out badly, but that's part of the game. If it was bound to work out rightly, it wouldn't be a speculation at all, and there wouldn't be the opportunities of profit that inhere in sound speculation."

That makes a lot of sense. He's saying that you need to experiment to find new things, and if you know the result ahead of time it's not an experiment! So you should not be afraid to take a chance and go for something new even if you don't know how your bet will turn out; just don't be stupid about it by going "all in" on one stock.

Instead you loading up on one big bet you can decrease the risk of losing money on any one stock by taking many small bets so that the diversification reduces the risk of any one stock causing serious harm.

So, as an example, if I just put a lot of money into one of those stocks I don't understand well then I'm speculating. But I can be intelligent about it, and diversify these by holding several risky things, which reduces the risk of the overall portfolio. Here's an example of a group of stocks where each one alone would be a kind of risky for me because I'm not an expert in any one of these companies, but since it's a diversified portfolio the overall risk of one company hurting me is small. Since each company is 10% of the portfolio, if one of suddenly dropped in price by 25% this would only lower the value of the portfolio by 2.5% which is something I could live with. Even a stock dropping by 50% would only lower the portfolio value by 5%. That is something most investors could survive.

If, however, you put all your money into that one stock that dropped 50% you would probably feel differently. Just remember to always be aware of when you're investing and when you're speculating, and it's okay to speculate as long as you're intelligent about it.

Here is a group of stocks that are speculative to me. For you, or any other investor, they might be businesses you understand well. I'm saying I don't have a deep knowledge of any one of these businesses.

A group of speculative stocks

1. Progressive (PGR)
2. Booz Allen Hamilton (BAH)
3. Illumina (ILMN)
4. Medtronic (MDT)
5. Seattle Genetics (SGEN)
6. T. Rowe Price (TROW)
7. Intuitive Surgical (ISRG)
8. Schlumberger
9. T-Mobile
10. Fortive

To keep investment and speculation separate in your mind, Graham says you should set aside a portion (the smaller the better) of your capital in a separate investing account for speculation, and says, "Never mingle your speculative and investment operations in the same account, nor in any part of your thinking."

One added benefit of making a separate investing account for speculation is that you have some "skin in the game"[6] by holding stocks you might otherwise only watch. When you're an owner of stock you'll pay more attention to a company's new products or services than a casual observer. You will receive annual reports so you'll keep updated on any new acquisitions, mergers, or future prospects. This means that if a company has the wind at its back you'll know sooner than if you were passively watching the company, and you will be more likely to make more investments at opportune times.

As a serious investor, I believe that using an established broker like Fidelity or Vanguard for your main account makes sense. For your "intelligent speculations" you can set up either a separate account with the same broker, use a different broker, or use an app like Robinhood app,[7] which seems to make sense for the money you earmark for intelligent speculation.

I like the idea of intelligent speculation because it gives you the chance to own stock even if you don't know exactly how things will work out. Remember that *there is intelligent speculation* just as there is *intelligent investing*, and the important thing is to be clear in your mind so you keep things clear in your mind.

Remember: don't speculate when you think you're investing, don't speculate seriously instead of occasionally as a pastime, and don't risk more money in speculation than you can afford to lose.

Saying "No" With Varying Degrees of Emphasis

At Berkshire Hathaway, Buffett explained that their decision-making process works like this: Buffett suggests ideas and Charlie says "no" emphatically.

"It would go like all our other conversations: He would say 'no' for about 15 minutes, and I would gauge by the degree, the amount of emotion he put into his 'nos' whether he liked the deal or not," Buffett said.

Not too long ago, Munger once said "no" to a very famous stock that everyone knows: Uber. Journalist Andy Serwer asked Munger, "As far as what's going on in Silicon Valley right now with IPOs, unicorns going public and not having any profitability or any prospect of profitability in the near term, what do you think of that situation?"

Munger replied, "Well, there are a whole lot of things that I don't think about and one of them is companies that are losing two or three billion dollars a year and going public—it's not my scene."

Serwer then asked, "Have you looked—so you're not interested in Uber or companies like that necessarily?"

"Well I have to be interested when they're that important and sweep the world and change practice, but I don't have to invest in everything I'm interested in. I'm looking for things where I think I can predict what's going to happen with a high degree of accuracy and I have no feeling that I have the ability to do that with Uber."

Munger doesn't even think about investing in Uber because he can't predict what's going to happen with the company, and like any smart investor, he doesn't gamble.

Stocks that I don't think about

Below are the stocks where I can't predict what's going to happen. At one point or another I thought they might be exciting to own, but I eventually said "no" to every single one of them.

Tesla - Elon Musk is a brilliant innovator. I love his ideas and his cars, but I don't have a clue if he can make Tesla profitable, and that's the only thing that matters to an investor: does the company make money, and will it continue to do so in the long term. Elon, please make cars and profits, not tweets!

Nvidia - Video game chips, self driving cars, but is the stock simply too expensive?

CVS - I remember CVS stores where I grew up in the Boston area as a kid. Since then I've seen the chain spread across the country like wildfire. I'm sure it's a well-run business, but I don't know enough about the pharmacy industry or this segment of the healthcare market to dip my feet in.

Uber - They own no cars and there is no barrier to prevent competition from entering this sphere and hurting their business. Also, they are far from profitable yet.

Square - Great payment processing, but I think any financial company could enter this market as there is no barrier to entry. Eventually another company could come along with better software or cheaper transaction fees and they could drink Square's milkshake.

Dropbox - Sure it's a useful service (one that I use myself), but it's only data storage with a nice user interface. Cloud storage is so inexpensive now and any company could come up with a better, cheaper solution and Dropbox could lose the pricing power they currently enjoy. It's hard to see how a company like this can innovate. They can make it easy for groups to collaborate or share images, text, or videos, but everyone can do that. Amazon and Google already offer competing storage for free, and if they were to decide to go "all in" on retail storage Dropbox would be toast.

Walt Disney - I think it's a great brand. They own Star Wars, Captain Marvel, ABC, Pixar, The Disney+ (the new video streaming service), Frozen, an arsenal of Disney classics, as well as Disneyland, Disneyworld, and all of the accompanying merchandising. And that's only a minuscule portion of what they own. But I'm less enthusiastic about their corporate leadership as the compensation for the CEO and top executives seems outlandishly exorbitant.

Texas Instruments - They make analog semiconductor chips, but what the hell do I know about those? I've heard that the company is well managed and has a wide moat, so while this could be an attractive prospect for an investor who understands semiconductors, this business is outside of my circle of competence.

Tencent - A dominant Chinese company. They own the major app, WeChat, used by more people in China than any other app. They also own the game "Honour of Kings". I know it's a fast-growing company that dominates Chinese culture, but I just don't understand the competitive forces in China well enough or the level of control the government could have over this company and its US investors.

Alibaba - I know it's the Amazon of China, but any company in China carries more risk than owning an American company. Why take all those risks to own the Amazon of China when you can own Amazon?

JD.com - The Craigslist of China. I know as much about rocket science as I do about JD.com. Hard pass.

Nike - Great sneakers, solid brand. But how does an already great company continue to innovate?

Lululemon - Worn by so many yoga practitioners and those who don't do yoga but want to look stylish. It's not inexpensive, this fashion statement for the upwardly mobile athletic woman - and they have lots of pricey pants and jackets for the men in their lives. But is the company well run, will their styles be relevant in five years, or will other fashion companies make them obsolete? And what about management? How well are they run now that their CEO was run out of town? So many questions, Lulu.

Five investing mistakes people make

1. Not buying stocks you know you should have
2. Buying stocks you know you shouldn't have
3. Selling stocks you should have held for years
4. Not buying more stocks during dips
5. Messing with options

Most success comes from saying "no" to bad ideas and not doing dumb things. It's as simple as that. In the words of Charlie Munger, "People are trying to be smart — all I am trying to do is not to be idiotic, but it's harder than most people think."

As you start looking at different stocks, start asking questions. If you don't know enough about the business, just say "no" and move on. You don't have to know everything, but knowing what you don't know is far more useful than being a genius.

SIX

INVEST

AT THE 2019 Berkshire Hathaway Annual Shareholder Meeting,[1] Warren Buffett told everyone that all investing can be explained by one of Aesop's most famous fables: "A bird in the hand is worth two in the bush."

Now, I want to say that I believe the meaning of this fable is different than Buffett's financial interpretation. I think the fable says you're better off with a sure thing than a better, yet uncertain thing.

Buffett's use of the fable is in comparing a sure investment (treasury bills that are considered "safe") with an investment in a company where there is uncertainty about (1) how much money the company will earn in the future and (2) when the company generates this cash. Having made the distinction between my interpretation and Buffett's let's hear why he believes the fable is useful to investors.

> "In the end, it all goes back to Aesop, who in 600 BC said, you know, that a bird in the hand is worth two in the bush. And when we buy Amazon, we try and figure out—the fellow that bought it—tries to figure out whether there's three, or four, or

five in the bush, and how long it'll take to get to the bush, how certain he is that he's going to get to the bush, and who else is going to come and try and take the bush away and all that sort of thing.

"A bird in the hand is worth two in the bush."

"And we do the same thing, and it really, despite a lot of equations you'll learn in business school the basic equation is that of Aesop and your success in investing depends on how well you are able to figure out how certain that bush is, how far away it is, and what the worst case is—instead of two birds being there only one being there—and the possibilities of four or five or 10 or 20 being there, and that will guide me, that will guide my successors in investment management at Berkshire, and I think they'll be right more often than they're wrong."

As you start seriously thinking about investing into a company, ask yourself whether the company will grow in the next three to five years. Can you see the runway for them innovating new products or finding ways to delight their customers?

You'll want to be able to write down (or explain to another person) how you see the "birds in the bush" and how they will emerge. How will the company continue to grow and increase their profits? You need to have confidence in the company's ability to grow.

For example, do you think Apple will come out with a better iPhone next time around? Or do you think they've lost their way? Do you see Facebook growing with some new innovations, or do you think their best days are long behind them?

What about Tesla? Are they going to dominate the electric car marketplace? Maybe several birds will fly out from the Tesla bush. But what if their competition makes better vehicles at cheaper prices? Maybe Tesla fails to achieve profitability and no birds emerge from the bush.

There's also the possibility that Tesla's share price drops so low that the entire business becomes so cheap that it becomes a takeover target for some tech company with deep pockets. What if Apple or Google buys Tesla? How many birds might emerge from the bush then? When will they emerge? Try to figure out the companies that may have many birds emerging in the next three, five, and 10 years, and consider investing in those.

One useful way to think about investing is asking yourself whether you personally prefer to own stock in a solid, reliable business or if you like taking chances and getting 'em when they're little? If you like taking more risk you might like buying stock in companies that have not yet become huge and successful.

All investing goes back to Aesop, and your job is to predict how many birds might be in that bush and when they'll emerge.

. . .

The market is there to serve you — not instruct you

Many investors spend a lot of time studying the market every day. They're glued to CNBC trying to figure out how the trade war, tariffs, changes in interest rates and the latest tweets will affect the market. They are trying to take their cues from the market; they are letting the market instruct them, and this is a big mistake.

The market is there to serve you, but not to instruct you. The proper approach is to focus on fundamentals of business, on the birds that may be in the bush, and when they will emerge. Most people focus on things beyond their control, like trying to predict the weather tomorrow. Nobody knows how to forecast the stock market or the weather with any certainty, so why even try.

If you can distance yourself from this idea that you need to pay attention to the stock market and react to it you'll be better off. Do your homework, understand businesses, and let the market serve you, on occasion, with attractive prices.

Not everyone should own stocks

Some people shouldn't own stocks at all because they just get too upset with price fluctuations. If you're gonna do stupid shit because your stocks go down, you shouldn't own stocks at all. Period.

Selling a stock because it goes down is one of the worst things you can do as an investor. You don't have to do anything just because the stock price goes down.

If you get nervous when the stock market gyrates you probably shouldn't invest. You will be a wreck worrying about what's happening, and you're more likely to take action at the worst possible time. For those with the patience and ability to withstand some turbulence, learning to invest will help you greatly over the long haul.

The long-term investing mindset

When I was a kid we used to talk about time capsules in school.

We never actually made one, but the idea of putting together a care package for the future that would be someone else's buried treasure stuck in my mind. Here's how it worked: you and your friends collect a bunch of items from your everyday life (some newspapers, photos, toys, recorded music, a cellphone, a takeout menu from a restaurant, and a handwritten letter for whoever opens the capsule) and put them in a waterproof container that you bury somewhere in hopes that someone 5, 10, 50 or 100 years in the future will dig up this capsule and discovers a slice of life from the objects provided.

I like the image because it captures the proper investing mindset of making a decision once and letting it sit, untampered with for many years. I'm not saying you should buy stocks and bury them in the dirt somewhere you'll never find them, but the idea that you'll have to commit to locking something away for many years and not messing with it is a good way to think about investing. You shouldn't care about the day to day stuff.

You should not even care if the stock market is open tomorrow or next week, because the daily quote shouldn't mean anything to you since you own parts of the company, and its success or failure over the next decade or two or three is what matters, not the daily price quotes.

I bought some shares of Carmax about eight years ago. The money I invested doubled in value in a few years. I just left it alone, didn't touch it. Now I just looked at it the other day and noticed that it has doubled *again*. My first investment had babies, and just a few years later those babies had babies. I've turned into a grandfather in eight years!

This Carmax example is a good way to think about investing. Just buy stocks in one (or a few) companies based on your research and bury them in your time capsule. Years later you might need a lot of money to put a down payment on a house, or buy a car, or pay for a kids' education. It will be there for you.

As a side note, don't literally forget about your stocks! Keep an eye on your[2] businesses from time to time and read their annual reports. Be like a parent who lets their kid ride their bike to school but reminds them to wear a helmet. You want to be mindful of safety but not a helicopter parent. If you did your homework in selecting the right stocks to begin with, everything else will be easy.

Own for the long term

The kind of investment you want to own is the one you can buy and hold for a long time without worrying about what's happening in the news, politics, or the stock market every day.

If you read financial news or watch CNBC you'll see daily commentary on what the stock market is doing as well as forecasts of questionable reliability about what will happen next. You'll see and read analyst reports on whether a company will meet or beat quarterly estimates. This is all short-term thinking, completely useless to the long-term investor. Brokerage firms, financial media, financial advisors, and all of Wall Street makes money telling you that you need to buy or sell something now based factors beyond your control. It's all bullshit.

If you have to follow a company closely, you shouldn't own it.

Short-term gambling mindset

Here's an example of the short-term gambling mindset.

The screenshot below is from the "Wall Street Bets" subreddit and it celebrates a large concentrated holding in Tesla stock just before an earnings announcement.

SMART STOCKS   81

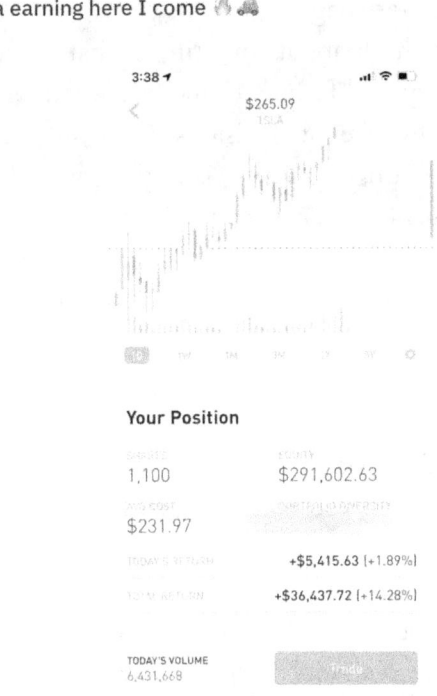

A typical "all in" trade from one of the do-it-yourself traders on the 900,000-user Reddit forum called r/wallstreetbets or r/WSB for short. Wall Street Bets traders typically share screenshots of their wild speculations trading stocks and options. Screenshot from Reddit Wall Street Bets.

This screenshot is a great example of what you don't want to do. The problem is that this is gambling, it's frivolous, and it celebrates the all-too-cavalier attitude that it's okay to lose.

There is nothing wrong with owning concentrated positions, but you should not look at them so closely, nor take such a "going all in" attitude in order to make a profit. Investing, when done right, should seem boring, unsexy, and not at all packed with the emotion and hustle of a Wall Street trading floor. Also, don't hedge your whole net worth on a single earnings release. That's an idiotic approach to managing your money.

. . .

Sit-on-your-ass Investing

The best way to think about investing is that it requires only a few good decisions in your lifetime. Embody the soul of a sloth when it comes to making investment decisions. Go slow, buy your stock, and sit back. Charlie Munger puts it this way:

"If you buy a business just because it's undervalued, then you have to worry about selling it when it reaches its intrinsic value. That's hard. But if you can buy a few great companies, then you can sit on your ass. That's a good thing."

Punch card with 20 slots

Warren Buffett thinks you can improve your results by limiting the number of stocks you buy in your lifetime. Charlie Munger describes it this way:

"When Warren lectures at business schools, he says, 'I could improve your ultimate financial welfare by giving you a ticket with only 20 slots in it so you had twenty punches – representing all the investments that you get to make in a lifetime. And once you've punched through the card, you couldn't make any more investments at all. Under those rules, you'd really think carefully about what you did, and you'd be forced to load up on what you'd really thought about. So you'd do much better.' "

Munger explained that the long-term holding period is the only way to go. "You're paying less to brokers, listening to less nonsense, and if it works, the tax system gives you an extra 1, 2, or 3 percentage points per annum."[3] In his mind, a portfolio of three companies is plenty of diversification.

"The idea of excessive diversification is madness," Munger said. "Our experience tends to confirm a long held notion that being prepared, on a few occasions in a lifetime, and to act promptly in scale...will often dramatically improve the financial results of that lifetime. All that is required is a willingness to bet heavily when the odds are extremely favorable, using resources available, as a result of prudence and patience in the past.

"It takes character to sit there with cash and do nothing. I didn't get where I am today, by going after mediocre opportunities. "If you say no to 90% of investing ideas, you're not missing much."

How do you get into these great companies?

Of course, if good businesses were easy to find, investing would be easy. Half the battle is finding these great companies at great prices.

How do you get into these great companies? One way is to find them when they're small, like buying Amazon when Jeff Bezos first took the company public. A lot of people try to do that, and it's mind-bogglingly hard because many companies are not successful at first. Amazon didn't make profits early on because they reinvested in their future and little companies that lose money don't always look like good investments. If you're young and have extra money to take a lot of chances, it might be worth trying out. But it's risky! You're essentially betting that one of these small companies will succeed. It's a gamble, so don't bet the farm!

Finding companies when they're small seems like a perfectly intelligent approach for somebody who has patience and the desire to learn about small companies. It's just not something that I've done.

But finding them when they're big is also hard because now everybody's doing it. What's the next Google, or Facebook, Microsoft, or Amazon? Well, nobody knows and that question gets harder to answer all the time.

Shoulda, coulda, woulda

Hindsight, as we all know, is 20/20. When I look back over the last 15 years I can see, clear as day, all the opportunities I've missed.

And they were big, juicy chances that were right before my very eyes. Instead of diving in (as I should have) I sat around sucking my thumb.

What happens is that I find a product I like, and my friends and I use it or buy it and think it's the coolest thing ever. It's not just us either; people all across the country (or even the globe) are having the same experiences as we are, and they're starting to get these sticky interactions with the product where they just can't put it down or stop using it. If you told them to they'd get upset and tell you to shove it.

Examples:

1. **Google:** Everyone started using this search engine and there was no turning back. Sure, you could use Bing, but nobody did unless they worked at Microsoft. Sure, go ahead and use DuckDuckGo to do your searches, my techie friends told me about it. Yet they still all use Google. You could have bought Google super cheap back in 2004 or 2005. People passed on Google stock back then when it was cheap, yet now they're buying it at $1,000+ a share.
2. **YouTube:** It was obvious this was the only video streaming game in town soon after Google bought it back in 2006. Everyone watched videos and there was no competition in this area, no runner-up video streaming services. So if you were watching hours of YouTube a week you could have figured millions of other people were getting addicted to the site as well. Yet I'd bet that a small percentage of YouTube addicts ever thought to buy Google stock. A big swing and a miss!
3. **Apple:** Everyone had iPods. Then these top-of-the-line MP3 players got really tiny and people loved them even more. Soon there was the iPod Shuffle, the iPod Touch, then the Holy Grail, the iPhone. There were all these devices that everyone had to own, but Apple

stock was not very popular at the time; it was dirt cheap. If you just look at the $20 stock price[4] when the iPhone was released in 2007, the Apple share price remained under $100 a share until the summer of 2014. That's seven long years when I could have bought this company I already knew was awesome at a cheap price.

4. **Amazon:** So many people I knew were buying tons of things on Amazon a decade ago. I just noticed that my first purchase on Amazon was in 2006. Yet I waited more than 10 years to buy stock in the company. I was going to that website first when I needed to buy something online. "Get it on Amazon" was a phrase I probably heard at least once a day. Did I buy Amazon stock in 2009 for $86? Nope. Did I know enough to realize the business was succeeding and more and more people were buying things on Amazon? Yup. Shoulda, coulda, woulda.

How do you find 'em small?

It's safe to say that if someone took away Google or YouTube or your iPhone you'd be pissed. Can you think of any companies that you use now that are winning your affections? What's something that you and your friends and family use a lot? Now go a tiny bit further and see if that business might be resistant to competition and if they're on track to be even more successful 10 years from now. Those might be the stocks you regret not buying a decade from now. Jump at these opportunities for companies you understand today so you can minimize future regrets.

Another way to find outstanding businesses when they're small is to ask yourself: "What product do I use that I wouldn't want to do without?" It could be a service or a website that if someone took it away you would protest. More importantly, you should be spending money on the service, or you should at least understand how it earns profits. You may not pay Google directly, but they get paid for clicks on ads and every video ad that you watch for more than 15 seconds. Just make sure the company is making money.

You might think that someone who writes a book about investing is always sure about the best thing to do all the time, but the truth is, sometimes I wonder if I'm doing the absolute best thing at any given time. I'll show you what I mean.

First, I just want to share with you the idea that at any point in time we are just a point on a curve. We may be at an all-time high or a low, but where you were exactly is only obvious years later. A lot of people try to figure out where we are on that curve, and if they think we are high up and about to crash, they sell. That market timing attitude strikes me as crazy — the idea that any one person can predict the future — it's like predicting rain a month from now. Also, if you go to cash now how will you know when to dive back into the market? Nobody will ring a bell for you!

So you have to make decisions on your own, and the problem is that sometimes you start to look at the market or the economy and then "do something" based on what you perceive. There's a lot of room for screwing up when you do this. Try not to make decisions based on where the market is, or what you predict might happen in the future. Look at the business and try to buy a quality business when the stock price is cheap compared to the outstanding business you're buying. This does occur periodically, and you just want to be ready. You don't need to forecast the economy.

I try to never buy stocks when the market is hitting new highs every day or week. It's so hard to resist buying stocks when everyone around you is excited and the prices just keep going up. I just have a pretty good investing temperament, and I'm decent at not giving in to these urges. Something seems to step in and stop me from doing dumb shit at the worst time. As you will recall from the earlier chapter I have made a couple awful mistakes, but it was because I didn't truly understand the business, and I try not to repeat that.

. . .

What if stocks seem expensive?

As of this writing the stock market has been on a long upward climb, and stocks are near all-time highs. If I were to plot a point on a line, the line would climb up, up, up and to the right with no major drop in sight. We're up in the clouds of high prices. There's no way to say if we've reached the top, or there's still more room to climb from here.

My plan most of the time is to stay 90% invested in stocks and 10% in cash. The simple reason for this is that I know over time that cash is going to return much less than stocks. Inflation gradually erodes the value of the dollar, so holding a lot of cash is not a smart strategy. The only reason you hold cash is to pay bills, buy stuff you need, and to take advantage of low stock prices. Otherwise holding a lot of extra cash makes little sense. It just becomes worthless over time.

So as the stock market continues to generate positive returns year after year, I can't help but think about some of the bad advice I've heard over the years. "take money off the table," or "rebalance periodically," or "don't put all your eggs in one basket." I remind myself that these are not intelligent people, and they're spouting ignorance and stupidity, also known as bullshit advice. Some of the advice comes from stock brokers and financial advisers whose salaries depend on the fees you pay when you make changes. The news media and talking heads on CNBC try to get you excited and make you think you have to watch your stocks and "do something" all the time. Most people who tell you what you should do now display their ignorance, not sophistication; they're not intelligent investors, they're clowns.

Jumping out of the market because you think it's high is tough, and the only thing that makes it even more difficult is that once you're out of the market you have to decide on the best time to jump back in.

Think about that — you have to correctly time getting out of the market and *then* decide when to buy back in with accuracy. That's *two* market timing decisions you have to make or you risk getting out too early or getting back in too late. If you don't time these decisions correctly then you risk jumping out of the market too early and missing a big run up in stocks — and even if you time that correctly and get out of the market before a crash, you must then decide when to jump back in. If you screw that up you can miss those first days of a bull market that are often characterized by huge gains. Miss those first few big up days and you won't participate in the early rebound because you were trying to time your re-entry, which is almost impossible to do.

What market crashes feel like

I remember all too well what it feels like when the market starts crashing. I witnessed this in 2000 and again in 2008. Usually it happens in a few big legs down[5], each can be 7% to 9% drops each day, and they're spaced out over a few months. The funny thing about crashing markets is that there are up days mixed in so you think that maybe everything's turning around and the decline is over... and then market drops again like a stone.

Crashes are unpredictable and gradually all of the optimists, traders, bulls, the people who thought they were in it for the long haul will have sold their shares. Once everyone swears off stocks, goes to cash, stuffs their money under the mattress, once the last person has sworn off stocks forever... that's when the market turns up again. But you never know when that moment occurs. You never know until a few weeks or months later, when you look back and realize that the storm is behind you and the sun has finally emerged once more. It's a pretty vicious shakeout though, and the manic change is obvious.

You'll be at a huge advantage, even if you've never personally experienced a gut-wrenching bear market, to know that one will happen sometime — they tend to happen once the bull market has been charging ahead for so long that everyone forgets that markets go down. They also end, so as long as you don't make stupid choices based on emotions you'll come out the other end just fine.

. . .

It's all about mindset

You have to be patient and wait until a stock comes along at a price that makes sense. That's an easy decision to make, but most people simply can't do it. It's contrary to human nature to sit around doing nothing. Most people can't wait when it comes to investing and they rush the process.

For most people, sitting on your ass for five years leaves most feeling restless and bored. They're not doing anything at all. But if there is nothing that makes sense to buy because prices are too high, not doing anything is the best thing you can do.

This quote by Munger will help you stay the course so you don't have to fear eventual, inevitable market declines. He said, "It is in the nature of stock markets that they go down. So people suffer then. Conservative investing and steady saving without expecting miracles is the way to go."

SEVEN

UNDERSTANDING

I WAS IN SANTA FE, New Mexico last week with my dad and on our last night in town we went to the Burrito Company for dinner. We were sitting in a booth and in the next booth over was a kid with his parents. We said hello when we sat down, but nothing after that.

As my dad and I were finishing up our dinner, the boy slid out of his booth and walked over to ours, flanked by his mother and father, who introduced us to their son Theo and told us that he had guessed my dad's age and wanted to see if he was right. So we said, "Sure, go for it." Right away, Theo said, "You're 13."

Theo was about 75 years off, but it didn't faze him at all. He was only six himself and he had a happy, relaxed, engaging presence. My dad asked him some questions about his family and Theo happily answered them all. When I asked him what his favorite food was he said, "Socks!" and then listed all the things that he puts on the socks he eats: ice cream, frosting, peanut butter, sprinkles, you name it. Some days he eats dirty socks, and sometimes clean. He was having so much fun recounting all the ways he prepares his socks; he had a vivid imagination to say the least.

We were all admiring this free spirit and his creative energy, and at that moment one question sprang to mind:

"How'd you get to be such a good kid?" I asked him.

"Because I'm ready," he said.

It was a spontaneous, unrehearsed answer that threw me off guard. Upon further reflection, though, it made sense. Theo was totally in the moment. There were no lines or lyrics or anything to remember, he's just 100% who he is and ready for whatever comes his way.

His attitude is such a winning way to approach life, always ready to handle whatever comes your way. The best way to do that is to accumulate as much wisdom as possible, and you can do that by reading.

Reading all the time will help you gain a better understanding of the world around you, and you'll start to see the patterns emerge that differentiate great companies from mediocre ones. This collage is comprised of 17 iPhone photos taken in a Barnes & Noble bookstore in Seattle. Shot, stitched, and colorized with the iPhone. Photo collage by Jeff Luke.

Get ready to pounce!

Reading and knowing a few companies really well will help you become a prepared investor. During good times when stocks are reaching new highs every day people forget that market crashes happen quickly. Being ready means that you know which stocks to buy, and you have cash ready to deploy. When the stock market falls quickly you may have the chance to buy stocks at a huge discount; sometimes these opportunities don't last long.

Therefore, if you spend some time getting ready for market declines, then you can patiently wait until a crash comes, or when there is a steep decline of 7% or 10% in a stock you understand. Once you have that bedrock of understanding done and you know the one, two, or three companies you want to buy, you'll be ready to pounce when they suddenly go on sale. Being decisive is much easier when you know what you're doing.

Why is understanding so important?

At this point you might be asking, "Why do I need to understand a business? Can't I just buy stocks and be done with it?" The answer is that you can get into trouble with stocks (which means losing money), especially if you borrow money to buy stocks. So you don't want to buy on margins, and you want to steer clear of the "get rich quick" fantasy.

Not all companies are created equal, and there are a lot of companies out there that are either not in good industries or are just mediocre companies. You'll want to skip over these companies and invest in those that dominate their industries, because their position will usually improve over time, and they will give you one good surprise after another — while the other companies will give you one difficult and painful decision to make after another (you'll be asking "Should I finally sell this dog now or just hold and prolong my suffering?").

If you want to find stocks that are better than average you must find ways your company is resistant to competition and can actually dominate their industry. If a company performs well over time, the stock eventually follows. This quote by Munger underscores the benefits of investing in great companies:

"A great company keeps working when you're not. A great company

will eventually earn more and more and more while you're just sitting and doing nothing. And a mediocre company won't do that. So you're harnessing a long-range force that will help you. It's very important. These mediocre companies, they by and large are going to cause a lot of agony and very modest profits. If you do fine, you've got to sell it and find another one. It's a lot of work. Whereas you just buy one great company, and if you get the right thing at the right price, you just sit there."

Helping with spelling and math

Several years ago I offered to mentor a local student with math, reading, and writing. I'd meet with Khunploy and her family and we'd go over her homework, I'd be helpful where I could, and I'd give her books to read that I thought would be useful. Somewhere along the line I decided to teach her about investing, a subject I never learned about in high school or college that I wish someone had taught me.

When Khunploy was about 10 years old I asked her to make a list of a few companies that she knew about for us to put into a stock portfolio that we could follow. It's the same challenge given to readers at the beginning of this book.

She wrote them down on a piece of paper, and after a few years of following the portfolio we input the data into an Excel spreadsheet so she could learn about spreadsheets and the portfolio would be updated automatically.

We followed her stocks, all the companies she understood because of where she lives and goes to school near Seattle. As you can see, some local companies like Microsoft (**MSFT**) and Nordstrom (**JWN**) made her list, as did Apple (**AAPL**) because she wanted to get an iPhone one day. The others, like Gap (**GPS**) and Coke (**KO**), she knew as a customer, and we added Berkshire Hathaway (**BRK.B**) because she knows about it through our conversations about investing.

Ticker Symbol	Price	10 shares	November 17 2011
MSFT	$25.54	$255.40	
AAPL	$377.41	$3774.10	
BRK.B	$74.30	$743.00	
JWN	$47.01	$470.10	
GPS	$19.25	$192.50	
KO	$66.62	$666.20	

Khunploy's stock portfolio outperformed the S&P 500 by a wide margin.

Khunploy's six stocks

This is a scan of the original piece of paper that Khunploy used to list stocks in her portfolio. As you can see, we bought 10 shares of each stock. Later we realized we could have invested equal dollar amounts into each stock, but this was just how we put it together at the time.

We invested in 10 shares of Microsoft (MSFT) at $25.54 per share, for a total of $255.40 invested.

We invested in 10 shares of Apple (AAPL) at $377.41 per share, for a total of $3,774.10 invested.

We invested in 10 shares of Berkshire Hathaway Class B (BRK.B) at $74.30 per share for a total of $743.00 invested.

We invested in 10 shares of Nordstrom (JWN) at $47.01 per share, for a total of $470.10 invested.

We invested in 10 shares of Gap (GPS) at $19.25 per share, for a total of $192.50 invested.

We invested in 10 shares of Coke (KO) at $66.62 per share, for a total of $666.20 invested.

Graph of returns after eight years

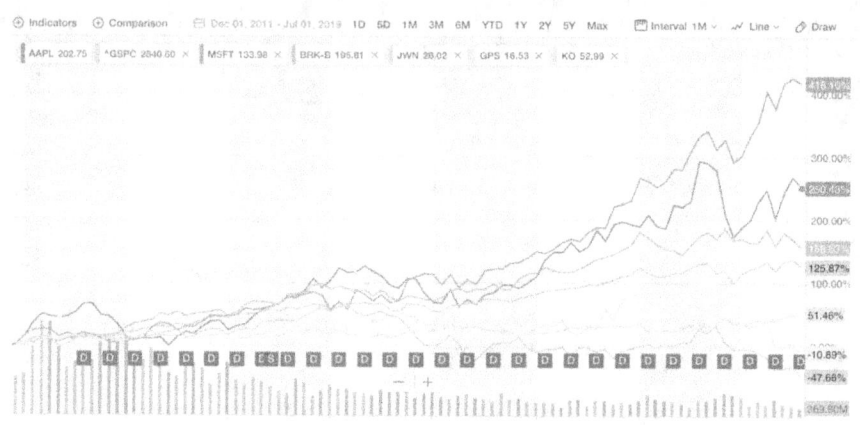

The initial amount invested on November 17th, 2011 was $6,101.30 and after eight years the total amount as of August 9th, 2019 was $17,877.08, so the total return during that time was 293%. During the same period, the S&P 500 returned 125.87%

Stock returns after eight years

Microsoft: We invested $255.40 and that investment increased by 416.10%, so we ended up with $255.40 (the original investment) plus an increase of $255.40 x 4.16, which is $1,062.72. So at the end we had a total of $1,318.12 which is $1,062.72 more than we invested.

Apple: We invested $3,774.10 and that investment increased by 250.43%, so we ended up with $3,774 (the original investment) plus an increase of $3774.10 x 2.5043, which is $9,451.48. In the end we had a total of $13,225.58, which is $9,451.48 more than we invested.

Berkshire Hathaway: We invested $743.00 and that investment increased by 156.63%, so we ended up with $743.00 (the original investment) plus an increase of $743.00 x 1.56.63%, which is $1,163.76. So in the end we had a total of $1,906.76, which is $1,163.76 more than we invested.

Nordstrom: We invested $470.10 and that investment decreased by -47.66%, so we ended up with $470.10 (the original investment) minus a loss of $470.10 x -.4766%, which is $224.05. So in the end we had a total of $246.05, which is $224.05 less than we invested.

Gap: We invested $192.50 and that investment decreased by -10.89%, so we ended up with $192.50 (the original investment) plus a decrease of $192.50 x -.1089% which is $20.96. So in the end we had a total of $171.54, which is $20.96 less than we invested.

Coke: We invested $666.20 and that investment increased by 51.46%, so we ended up with $666.20 (the original investment) plus an increase of $666.20 x .5146, which is $342.83. In the end we had a total of $1,009.03, which is $342.83 more than we invested.

The total returns more than doubled the S&P 500

The initial amount invested on November 17th, 2011 was $6,101.30 and after eight years the total amount as of August 9th, 2019 was $17,877.08, so the total return during that time was 293%.

During the same period, the S&P 500 returned 125.87%.

Take home lesson

Not only can you survive with a portfolio that is not diversified over a long period of time, you can double the stock market average if you stick to what you understand.

You also can "just sit back and do nothing" as you can see from this example. Nothing was added and nothing was taken away from this collection of six stocks.

Looking at the final returns of the six stocks, one could easily say that just selling the Gap and Nordstrom stocks would have improved the total returns. But hindsight is perfect, and in the early years one of the other stocks could have experienced a long period of underperformance. You can meddle too much with a portfolio, and these results show that you don't have to have a portfolio with 50 or 100 stocks to do well, and you don't have to jump in and out of the market either.

Understanding is your first hurdle

One thing I like about Khunploy's portfolio is that it was made up only of companies she knew and admired. She stuck to what she understood.

Speaking of sticking to what you understand, Warren Buffett once said, "If you find three wonderful businesses in your life you'll get very rich. And if you understand them...bad things aren't going to happen to those three. That's the characteristic of it."[1]

The other aspect of these six stocks that really helped returns is that a large amount of the early investment went into Apple, Berkshire, and Microsoft, and all of those companies performed extremely well. Had a larger amount gone into the Gap or Nordstrom the total returns would have been worse. Investing a lot in her best ideas paid off well over the first eight years with these stocks.

"Know what you own"

Peter Lynch[2] thought that to "know what you own" was the "single most important thing" for investors. He quickly followed it up with: know why you own it.

It seems simple enough, but how many people truly take the time to understand a company before they buy it? In my personal observations, people often buy stocks based on something they overhead in casual conversation or something they read online. There is often an aspect of excitement in the decision to buy stock. But what's lacking here is understanding.

We have a world of information at our fingertips, but I doubt much has changed since Lynch uttered those words over two decades ago.

At a speech during a Press Club Luncheon in 1994, Lynch said, "And the single most important thing to me in the stock market, for anyone, is to know what you own. I am amazed at how many people own stocks, they would not be able to tell you why they own it. They couldn't say in a minute or less why they own it. Actually, if you really press them down, they'd say, 'The reason I own this is the sucker is going up.' And that's the only reason. That's the only reason they own it. And if you can't explain—I'm serious, if you can't explain to a 10-year-old in two minutes or less why you own a stock, you shouldn't own it. And that's true I think of about 80% of people that own stocks."

"I made money in Dunkin' Donuts," Peter Lynch said. "I can understand it." The most important thing in the stock market is to "know what you own," he said. "You want to invest in stocks you can understand, and if you don't understand it you should avoid it," he said. One of Lynch's main piece of advice to investors is you should be able to say in a minute or less why you own a stock. *Photo by Jeff Luke*

"I made money in Dunkin' Donuts," Lynch said. "I can understand it. When there was recessions I wouldn't have to worry about what was happening. I could go there, people were still there, I didn't have to worry about low-priced Korean imports. I mean, I just didn't have—you know, I could understand it. And you laugh. I made 10 or 15 times my money in Dunkin' Donuts."

You want to invest in stocks you can understand, and if

you don't understand it, you should avoid it; this is the single biggest principle that so many people ignore when they buy stock. People are often so careful with their money, they'll spend hours researching a digital camera online or a week searching for the best airfare for a trip to Croatia or Thailand. Then they hear about a new pot stock, cryptocurrency or a faux beef company and they spend hundreds or thousands of dollars betting that the stock will go up. Yet they don't understand the company, they don't even know if it's making a profit. The excitement of a high stock price is all it takes to get people excited. These things can can and will end badly.

If you want to build a deep understanding of businesses, think of yourself as an investigative reporter; ask a lot of questions, take notes, and try to create a picture of the business. Figure out who the competition is, and this company's position in relation to others in its industry. Learn about the company's leaders, its future, and any obstacles it may face in the road ahead.

Tools to help you understand

To help you in your quest to understand businesses, I'd like to share with you two services that I find useful.

Morningstar

Morningstar offers both a free and premium service. I used the free service for a few years until I got a chance to use the premium service, which is more useful. The premium service provides financial analyst summaries of companies that will help you understand the business and its competitors.

The Morningstar analyst summaries have some useful information in them about each business they cover. They discuss valuation (whether they think the stock is cheap, selling at a fair price, or expensive) and they also note whether they believe the company possesses a moat.

Seattle residents with library cards can access the Morningstar analyst database free of charge. If your library offers access for free, I recommend this way of reading their reports. Otherwise I wouldn't pay for the service.

Value Line

Another useful resource is Value Line, which provides excellent surveys of many different US companies. These are summaries that discuss the company's financial strength, their relative strength within their industry, and the way the company could be affected by various economic factors. Value Line surveys are a great way to learn about a business and read the company's financials.

Value Line also provides "timeliness" ratings for stocks, but I think you should ignore them. In my opinion these numbers are not reliable indicators of where the stock price is going. Beware of anyone who claims to know where the stock price may go in the future; forecasting is a fool's game. Remember that the people writing these reports are not making their salaries largely as investors (they make money by researching and writing), so the success of their recommendations should always be taken with a heaping serving of salt.

I believe these summaries are a great way to learn about companies. In Seattle, you can use the library's free database to use Value Line with a library card. If you can access Value Line from your library's free database, I think you'll enjoy reading through Value Line's surveys. They would be worth the subscription for the useful investing information alone.

Problems with financial analyst summaries

There are many problems with reading research provided by

financial analysts. In short, you may understand the businesses they describe better than they do.

The problem, as I see it, is that analysts focus too much on the balance sheet and tangible assets instead of income statements and other hard-to-quantify aspects like the future, the brand, and the business' competitive strength within its industry. It's tempting to focus on financial analysis, but if you pay too much attention to the numbers you'll risk making the mistake of those who "can't see the forest for the trees." Financial numbers capture some aspects of a business such as revenue, income, and expenses, but they can't help you judge the staying quality of the business in terms of its competitive advantage.

The other problem is that analysts look mainly at data like revenues, income, expenses, earnings per share, and price-to-earnings ratios to decide whether to recommend a stock. They suffer from the problem that Charlie Munger describes when he says, "People calculate too much and think too little."

Your understanding may lead you to see why a company has a high likelihood of success over the next several years while an analyst gets stuck on whether the company will be successful in the next quarter.

Analysts are incentivized to determine earnings within a few cents in a short timeframe. Your goal should be with a much longer time span. The analyst has short-term time pressures, and you can sit back and see how everything fits together. You can see the forest.

Furthermore, analysts come in two basic stripes: buy-side and sell-side. The buy-side analysts work for mutual fund companies and other financial institutions and work to decide which securities to buy. The sell-side analysts work for Wall Street brokerage firms and others who underwrite stock offerings and their analysis is geared toward selling securities.

"In the corporate world, if you have analysts, due diligence, and no horse sense, you've just described hell." — Charlie Munger

I do believe reading the Morningstar and Value Line analyst

summaries are a good way to get background on a company, so if you're just getting started learning about a company their summaries are a good place to start, but I wouldn't pay attention to the buy or sell recommendations that accompany the summaries.

Also ask yourself this: "If analysts are so smart, why are they sharing this information with me?" If they were really brilliant about stocks, they'd borrow as much money as possible from family and friends, buy their best stock ideas, and get fabulously rich. The reality is they can't make money off their ideas. The information isn't all that valuable. Analysts get paid by the brokerage firms that hire them. So don't worship their advice.

Read annual reports

One of the best things you can do to gain a powerful understanding of a company is read the annual report, which you can easily search for online and download. I recommend reading a few of them, not just the most recent one.

The annual report is the document that the company publishes to inform you about the business over the course of the past year; the highs, the lows, any acquisitions, stocks they bought or sold, share repurchases, etc. It's a way the company explains to you everything you need to know as an owner (or prospective owner) of the company.

Read the letter to shareholders

I personally like to read the letters to shareholders, written by the CEO, that discuss the business' activities for the past year and what to expect for the future. It's written in a conversational tone so a reader without a financial background can follow it. These letters should give you an idea of where the company has been and where it hopes to go in the future. I think that reading the annual report is the best starting point to gaining an understanding of a company, and I'm amazed by how many people buy stock in a company without first reading this free and information-packed report.

Along with reading the annual report (downloading it takes less than a minute, so there's no reason not to) I like to watch YouTube videos that feature interviews with the CEO. I will usually click on a few until I find one I really like, and I'll just watch 10 minutes or so, and if it's really good and I'll watch the whole thing. It's a great way to "get a feel" for whether you like the way the company's leader thinks and expresses themself.

I've watched some videos where I had no sense of trust or connection with the CEO, and others I've watched all the way through with a great sense of admiration. Those are the CEOS that give me a sense of confidence that they know what they're doing and can be trusted. It's such a simple way to filter out businesses and figure out which ones you like. I'm surprised more people don't do this, but now you know how useful watching a video interview can be, so you can do it yourself.

Two useful stock apps

StocksTracker

I like the StocksTracker app for iPhone and Android, since it lets you set up many different watchlists so you can follow as many stocks as you like. I enjoy setting up several different watchlists depending on which stocks I'm thinking about buying. This helps me to quickly scan the stocks and their price movements over time.

StocksTracker is useful as a quick way to get a sense of what the market is doing from day to day. I want to caution you that you can't truly learn anything from these stock price movements. You will be much better off learning about businesses by reading articles, books, and annual reports.

However, I think it makes sense to know when a company's stock gets cheap, and if you have the stocks you follow on watchlists in the app you'll be able to see their prices quickly and easily in one place.

There is a free version of the app and a paid one. I have used the free app and it works fine except for the slightly bothersome ads that show up when you first open the app. You can pay for an "ad free" app, but I have heard that the paid app is actually buggy and not an improvement, so I stick with the free version since it works well.

Robinhood

While I have never personally signed up for Robinhood, I think any app that gives a user a chance to dip their toes into the world of investing makes sense. It used to be that only rich people with a lot of money could afford brokerage accounts, and the fee per trade was about $100. Fast forward about 20 years and costs per trade went down to $10 and then $5 and now with Robinhood they're free.

The simple benefit to Robinhood is that you can invest at no cost to you, and you can follow your stock and learn more about the business by participating as an investor. There is really no way to learn about some things than by doing. In my 20s, when I started out as an investor, the minimum to open a mutual fund account was $1,000 and additional investments had a $100 minimum. With the ease of making trades on a smartphone, investing has never been easier, or cheaper.

There's no magic formula

Sorry to say, but there isn't a single magical investing formula that will let you rake in Scrooge McDuck levels of money. You need to know about business and human nature, and you have to be good at looking beyond numbers to get a feel for the qualities that set a company apart. When you find good qualities in a company, like a great leader and a sensible stock price, you're well on your way to true understanding.

EIGHT

MOAT

AN INVESTING MOAT IS A BUSINESS' ability to resist competition and protect its long-term profits. A strong brand, unique product, or superior service create a moat around a business that makes it very difficult for competitors to break in and peel away some of the company's customers, just as a moat defends a castle against attacks.

You want to buy stock in a few outstanding businesses and not worry about their ability to earn profits for years to come. If you invest in businesses that have these "moats" you won't have to worry about your investment from year to year. You can just buy the stock, sit back, and kick your feet up.

The following drawing shows Bob, The King of Squirrels, flanked by bodyguards in ninja hoodies who protect the castle and its prized stash of acorns. A hungry alligator patrols the moat, ready to devour any creatures who try to swim across. The hungry squirrel and its beaver companions are trying to figure out how to cross the moat to get acorns.

A moat is a deep, wide ditch filled with water that surrounds a castle to defend itself against attacks from invaders. Moats around businesses are protective barriers that make it hard for competitors to duplicate a company's success and take away their market share. Strong brands, products, services, and cultures all contribute to the strength of moats, and great companies continually look for ways to widen them.

A wide range of companies like Nike, Apple, Coke, Disney, McDonald's, Home Depot, Costco, Google, Boeing, Microsoft, Starbucks, and Amazon all have wide moats that protect their businesses. Most companies either have no moat or a narrow moat, so a wide moat is a powerful attribute.

Starbuck's moat is the consistency of its cafe experience no matter what country you're in, the many locations of its stores across the world, and the growing power of the Starbucks brand and its recognizability across the world, from the USA to South America, Europe, Brazil and China.

Berkshire Hathaway owns many companies with moats, such as GEICO, which offers low cost car insurance. Car insurance is considered a commodity by many people, and GEICO's moat is being the lowest cost provider.

Amazon's moat is the company's customer obsession. It provides the selection, price, and fast delivery at a level that's never existed before. If you wanted to start your own online retailer and try to outcompete Amazon you probably couldn't do it. That's the effect of a wide moat.

Moats are dynamic

The moat surrounding a business is dynamic. Few businesses are content to have a static moat, and the best companies are continually widening their moat by providing new products or services, a cheaper product or service, or strengthening the customer bond. In this chapter we'll look at Coke, Pepsi, Microsoft, Apple and GEICO and see why each company has a moat. One important question I want you to ask when looking at a company is whether the moat is getting wider or narrower. All great businesses have leaders who find ways to widen the moat and protect their fortress.

To grasp why this is such an important distinction, you really want to buy stock once and forget about it.[1] Since you only want to have to make one buy decision and not have to look at the stock and wonder if you should sell it, you should aim to buy stock in a business that's widening the moat, and not one where the moat is shrinking.

As an example of how you need to dig a bit to find out if a moat is shrinking or widening, let's look Coca-Cola, McDonald's and Starbucks. I've read and heard a lot in the media about about people making "healthier" choices which seem to suggest that consumers are drinking fewer soft drinks and eating fast food less often. Do these statements correspond to the data? I researched the stock price returns of Coca-Cola, McDonald's, and Starbucks over the past three-, five-, 10- and 15-year periods[2] compared to the S&P 500 index. Keep in mind these are relative results, meaning they show the extent to which each company's stock has outperformed the "average" US company. Stock prices are not perfect indicators of business success, but when a company does well its stock price generally follows. Here are the stock price returns for these three companies:

1-year returns

- Coca-Cola: 19.00%
- McDonald's: 33.11%
- Starbucks: 62.17%

3-year returns

- Coca-Cola: 11.38%
- McDonald's: 23.96%
- Starbucks: 20.72%

5-year returns

- Coca-Cola: 7.79%
- McDonald's: 19.38%
- Starbucks: 20.14%

10-year returns

- Coca-Cola: 9.44%
- McDonald's: 15.58%
- Starbucks: 25.03%

It's worth noting is that Coca-Cola has had lagged the performance of Starbucks and McDonald's over all time periods shown above.

Coca-Cola's moat may be narrowing for a variety of reasons. Its relative performance was more robust in previous decades, but consumer tastes may be changing. It's difficult to know for sure, but Coke may be vulnerable if people start to choose "healthier" alternatives. Not only is Coke underperforming relative to McDonald's and Starbucks, it's losing to the S&P 500 as well.

It's hard to know what, exactly, accounts for Coke's underperformance relative to the S&P 500, but I would guess that their competition is cutting into their profits. More people may be drinking Juice, LaCroix water, Kombucha, Red Bull, Smoothies, or going to Starbucks. Whatever the reason, the market is not as excited about Coca-Cola over the last decade as it had been in the past.

McDonald's and Starbucks seem to be growing their businesses faster than Coca-Cola and also widening their moats. You can easily find the total stock returns for any company with a quick online search useful to see if a company's is performing well over long periods of time (especially 5- and 10-year periods) to see if the moat is widening or narrowing.

You want to stack things in your favor before you invest, and you can do this by searching for companies with moats that will protect them in the future like the moats around McDonald's and Starbucks. You don't need to own stock in many businesses like those to get rich.

Which companies will win?

The key to investing is *not to guess if an industry* will benefit society, or how fast it will grow, but *which company within the industry* will have a competitive advantage and how long that will last.

Let me share two examples:

1. *Electric cars* – I have no doubt that electric cars, or gas/electric hybrids will only increase in popularity. If I were to invest in this area I would want to be able to predict, with a high degree of certainty, which company would have an advantage over all the others. Tesla gets constant media attention for obvious reasons, and especially because Elon Musk has become a celebrity and Tweets regularly.

But is it possible that already established auto makers could dominate the electric or hybrid industry? It could be that Tesla could run out of money or somehow make critical mistakes that doom the business. I would say that it is difficult to know at this early juncture who will dominate the electric car industry. The existing car makers (BMW, GM, Ford, Porsche, Volkswagen, Honda and Toyota) already have profitable businesses.

You can assume that they have engineers taking apart Teslas and examining every detail of the hardware and software used, and trying to figure out how to improve upon the design. These car manufacturers already have plants, employees, and processes in place.

Again, this is nothing against Tesla or its leader, it's just an observation; there's no way to know with certainty if Tesla will have a competitive advantage in electric cars five or 10 years from now. They may be just one of many companies making electric cars, and they may have no moat, and be constantly struggling to keep up with competition. On the other hand, if they do have the "secret sauce" of electric vehicle creation and production, then they could become dominant electric car maker and widen their moat. It's still too early to know for sure.

2. *Mobile Phones* – Among my cohort the iPhone is the mobile device that most people aspire to own, and it was clearly the first mobile device to combine music, photos, video, Internet browsing and email in one package with an app store in one small package with excellent design. The question I would have about investing in Apple is this: is Apple's moat, which is wide due to customer loyalty, going to continue to grow, or are the company's best days in the past and its moat is shrinking?

I believe Apple will survive the flood of competition over the next several years because it has so many loyal users, and a stickiness to Apple products, and most loyal customers will not want to switch to another phone. The company is the most profitable smartphone maker on the planet[3] and they have stockpiled a lot of cash to fund research & development. Even if they don't innovate as they have in the past, it seems as though their current customers will buy again and again[4], and that gives the company a moat, though I don't think it's a wide moat. It seems narrow at the moment due to competition, and it's anyone's guess if Apple's moat is widening or shrinking.

Apple faces steep competition from Samsung and Huawei, whose phone sales have been growing faster than Apple or Samsung's[5]. It's anyone's guess how much worldwide competition Apple will face from these new phones, but there is a possibility that the competition could innovate more quickly and bring new technologies to their devices before Apple.

One aspect of Apple's current moat is that the company is a luxury brand, and many people who buy iPhones either consciously or unconsciously are signaling their good taste or financial status by paying top dollar for their phones. That is a huge plus for Apple, because it ensures loyalty from this segment of customers, and knowing that someone will likely buy future devices from you (iPads, MacBooks, iWatches, iPods, etc) is a huge wind at your back.

But the question for an investor is whether this moat is widening, or whether things are going to get more difficult for Apple in the future as the advantage that the company had with Steve Jobs and

Jony Ive[6], the outgoing chief design officer of Apple, will disappear. The innovation and design of future iPhones are in the hands of new people, and it is uncertain whether the pace of invention will continue and Apple's moat will persist.

Competitors are not enemies

It's worth asking whether two companies seem like competitors can both have moats. At first glance, it looks like Apple and Microsoft are competitors. Does this mean that one of them has a moat and the other doesn't? It's a good question and worth digging a bit for the answer.

Both companies have competed with one another in the past (the hot debate of "Which is better, Mac or PC?" but that competition does not affect their moats in the competitive market. Sure, some people will prefer one operating system over the other for video games, writing, coding or doing Photoshop work, but those are specific niches for individual users and people tend to gravitate toward the system that works best for their specific needs.

If you look at the Latin root of "competition" you'll see it comes from the Latin roots "com-" meaning "with" and "petere" meaning "to seek." Put together they form the Latin word "competere," which means to strive together. Competitors can strive together without being enemies, and this seems to be the case with Apple and Microsoft which are both wide moat tech companies. One of them can grow and innovate without directly harming the other. There are some areas where companies compete directly – for example Microsoft for years has attempted to popularize a Windows phone, but without much success. If this device had taken off then Microsoft would be a strong competitor with Apple in the smartphone category. But that never happened and Apple is primarily a device company and Microsoft sells software.

. . .

Apple and Microsoft

Apple and Microsoft both have moats, but they're different moats. Apple's special bond is through selling devices and apps to retail customers, and Microsoft's bond is selling software to corporate customers. Each company can widen its moat without harming the other.

Apple is the dominant smartphone maker by making quality devices, and creating the iPhone, which has become such a powerful status symbol that communicates the success and desirability of its owner to others.

Microsoft dominates corporate America's operating system software. Other companies have tried to drink their milkshake (Linux, for example) but failed. I have not seen any software companies that pose a serious threat to Microsoft's dominance.

iPhones say "Mate with me!"

Apple dominates Smartphone makers, as the iPhone is more than just a phone, it's a status symbol. It shows the world that you have money and are successful, and this widens a company's moat.

NYU professor Scott Galloway sees Apple as a luxury brand like Louis Vuitton, characterized by an iconic founder and "temples to the brand" (Apple Stores).[7] He says that people use their iPhones to signal their desirability to others.

"Your No. 1 instinct is survival and, once that box is checked and you think, 'I'm going to make it through the day,' your No. 2 instinct is procreation," Galloway said.[8] "The No. 1 signal of wealth, the No. 1 signal of power, the No. 1 signal of your likelihood of a random sexual encounter in a greater selection set among potential mates is the iPhone."

Galloway says that and iPhone is a new signaling device. "An iPhone is saying to the opposite sex, or a potential mate, 'I have good genes. You should mate with me,'" Galloway said.

Apple's moat may be widening as they gain more loyal customers.

For quite a while, it seemed as though the iPhone cohort did not want a low-priced phone to replace their iPhone when the time came for a new one. Virtually all iPhone users replaced their existing iPhone with another iPhone. There are not a lot of retail products like that, where loyalty is almost guaranteed. There are iPads and MacBooks and Apple watches, but those are extra products that round out Apple's world, but the company basically lives and dies by the iPhone now.

Whether this will continue indefinitely is anyone's guess. I believe that going forward, Apple's success will depend heavily on the iPhone and not the iWatch, iPods, iPad, or MacBooks. The company is well-capitalized and not likely to disappear anytime soon, but whether they will continue to widen their moat by improving their iPhones and keeping customers loyal reminds to be seen. Some articles suggest that some iPhone users are dumping iPhones and buying Samsung. I have not seen this happen, but it doesn't mean it's not so. I think a potential investor in Apple should take a close look at whether its dominance seems assured for the next decade, and ask if the businesses' moat is widening or narrowing[9].

Some say the iPhone isn't necessarily the best smartphone. The best Android phones, some could argue, are out-designing the iPhone. Devices like Samsung's Galaxy S8 have features that just aren't available on Apple's flagship phones. Yet Apple is far in front and owns the lion's share of the smartphone industry's profits: iPhone owners are far more loyal than any Android owners.[10] According to a recent Morgan Stanley survey by Statista, 92% of iPhone owners who plan to get a new phone in the next 12 months say they're "somewhat or extremely likely" to stick with Apple. That trend, if it continues into the future, bodes well for Apple's moat.

The iPhone is an iconic device. Customers from China, Australia, Africa, Brazil and Israel may speak different languages, but they all share a common tool of communication, the iPhone, and they will go to great lengths to get one. As evidenced by the long lines outside Apple Stores in the United States, the demand is powerful.

People in other countries go great lengths to get iPhones, and pay much higher prices in their currencies. The iPhone is a luxury device, a status symbol, an Internet device, a music player, and a personal computer — all in a package that fits in the pocket.

The Apple App Store continues to widen Apple's moat by making it easier for developers to make money by creating apps which are useful to iPhone users. The ease and ubiquity of Apps make them like tiny little drug deals dishing out dopamine hits to the masses. Some people have only 5 apps on their phone, while some have 50 or 500. These apps are continually updated, with new ones released every day, and combined they make up an ecosystem that's unmatched in the smartphone world.

Microsoft: boring, yet consistent

Microsoft is not nearly as sleek or sexy as Apple, but they are not appealing to the retail customer. Instead they create a boring product that people who work for businesses need to create and edit documents and presentations. Their products are as plain vanilla as they get, but they produce a consistent product that works and offers a high level of compatibility when sharing documents online. Microsoft offers consistency to its corporate customers around the world.

Microsoft had a period of stagnancy where people disliked its software, phones, and everything it touched. The company has its fingers in many pies, trying to (unsuccessfully) sell a Windows phone and also a personal assistant, Cortana, in what looks like a hail-Mary attempt to keep up with Apple's Siri.

With former CEO Steve Ballmer out of the picture, Microsoft is finding new success under CEO Satya Nadella who has reinvigorated Microsoft with Azure, the company's cloud services segment.

Azure has been a game-changer for Microsoft, and Azure now makes up 30% of Microsoft's revenues. In a few short years Microsoft under Nadella became a fast-growing cloud services company, and they did so blowing by Google to make it a two horse race with

Amazon Web Services (AWS) which is still the #1 force in cloud computing. The Windows operating system remains Microsoft's cash cow, but Azure is quickly becoming Microsoft's other source of strength and further widens Microsoft's dominance in the corporate software market.

Two tech competitors with moats

Apple and Microsoft compete in the field of computer hardware and software without being enemies. The companies both have moats, and each grows its own moat without destroying the other.

Apple can succeed by innovating and coming up with better iPhones without damaging Microsoft (except the possibility that Microsoft will have to scrap the Windows phone if nobody buys them!)[11]

Microsoft can succeed by improving Windows operating system, Word, Excel, Powerpoint, and improving its Azure cloud services.

Both Apple and Microsoft are competitors in that they both have their own operating systems and software, but the success of one company does not directly harm the other, and while there is some overlap in their customers, their moat is in the devices and software that fill vastly different needs.

Coke & Pepsi's moats

Two competing companies like Coca-Cola and Pepsi can each have moats. Coke has more loyal customers, better beverage market share, higher profit margins, and greater presence in restaurants and stores around the world.[12] Coke is leader worldwide when it comes to soft drinks.

The ubiquity of the Coca-Cola brand make it one of the most recognizable brands on the planet, and are the basis for the company's wide moat. You could buy stock in Coke and just forget about it, and know that the company will be around 10 or 20 years from now

— just as it has since 1892. There is no sure way of knowing if the moat is widening or shrinking, but it does exist.

Pepsi's also has a wide moat, but it's mainly attributable to the company's food business. Snacks like Doritos, Lays Potato Chips and Quaker Oats drive about half of Pepsi's revenue and contribute more profit to the bottom line than Pepsi's beverage arm, mainly because of Frito-Lay's market dominance — because Frito-Lay has about 25% of the global market share of the potato chip market, compared to single-digit share for competitors.

So while Coca-Cola is the first name in soft drinks, Pepsi is most profitable selling chips in grocery stores and convenience stores and at gas stations, and that enhances the brand and gives Pepsi its wide moat.

GEICO's moat

GEICO sells car insurance, something that most customers view as a commodity. Everyone needs car insurance, and it's hard to tell the difference between insurers. You already know that GEICO's moat is that it offers the cheapest insurance, they remind you in every ad that if you call their toll-free number you'll probably find that you can save 15% on car insurance.[13]

When you start looking at companies you're considering as stock investments, keep your eyes open to the different qualities that make a moat. Amazon is so devoted to customers that it's often the first place they look when they need a great price and want something delivered fast. Apple makes beautifully designed technology that tells other people you've got taste.

GEICO is the lowest-cost insurance. Look for companies that are so good at what they do that you know you can just buy the stock and not have to look at it for 10 or 20 years because the company is so good at what it does, and has such loyal customers that they will succeed without you having to check up on them every day, week, month or week. Companies with moats make your decision easy, and they deliver one present surprise after another instead of one problem after another.

The Darwinian struggle

Businesses usually begin small, often selling one product or service, and with time they either grow to dominate their niche and become a fringe player, or they fade into obscurity. If you can find the businesses that will dominate their industry for years to come you'll be at an enormous advantage.

Competition is tough; each company engages in a vicious Darwinian struggle for survival. Every company tries to produce a product or a service that will attract customers and their dollars. And every business strives to come up with better products for their customers to buy. Even the best companies cannot afford to become complacent; they have to stay one step ahead of the competition always nipping at their heels, always trying to make better and cheaper products and deliver them faster.

Just look at the iPhone. It's one of the most popular smartphones in the world[14], and as anyone who owns one, or has family or friends who own one, it's a sticky product. What I mean by that is that when an iPhone user is ready to buy a new smartphone in a few years, there's a high likelihood that they'll buy another iPhone.

That kind of brand loyalty gives Apple a moat. It means if they can get a large number of people into their ecosystem and buying their iPhones (and chargers, cables, and other dongles), then they can continue selling them more devices in the future. If you imagine the company being a castle, the tendency of customers to stay loyal to Apple provides the moat.

Competitors nipping at your heels

Even terrific companies like Apple have to put forth a lot of effort in staying ahead of the curve. As successful as the iPhone has been, there is no guarantee that it will be the dominant phone 10 or 20 years from now. Steve Jobs set a high bar for innovation, but it's unclear if his successors will be able to continue to innovate at the rapid pace that it did under its founder.

As you read this, companies like Google, Huawei and Samsung are making great strides to take away iPhone market share. In fact, the Samsung Galaxy Note 10+ , the Samsung Galaxy S10 Plus are all giving the iPhone XS Max steep competition. The wide moat that Apple enjoys with its iPhone could start to narrow quickly if the company slips up, or even fails to innovate as quickly as its competitors.

Amazon made an attempt to break into the smartphone market with the Fire Phone, and though that was not a success, one cannot count Amazon out of the smartphone game just yet.

While Apple has a moat around their business (their iPhone franchise) there is no way to know for sure that this moat will endure a heavy siege. It seems safe for now, but the corporate highway is strewn with the roadkill of companies that didn't keep up with the competition.

Companies with moats dominate

Another way to think of a moat is a durable competitive advantage. It is what makes your company the top dog. Every sector of the economy usually has a company with a wide moat; the food and beverage industry has Coca-Cola, McDonald's, and Starbucks.

If a company lacks a moat then it's likely to suffer huge injuries when new companies burst through the castle walls. Earnings can fall short, new competitors will steal your customers, and your stock will crash 25% in a day because the business was not resistant to competition. Leo Tolstoy's Anna Karenina begins: "All happy families are alike; each unhappy family is unhappy in its own way."

The same would be said of happy businesses; they enjoy pleasant earnings surprises, grow their businesses, and widen their moats.

Each unhappy business is unhappy in its own way, losing money and losing customers because they are vulnerable to competition without a moat.

Finding moats

My goal is to teach you how to find moats on your own. You can, of course, take the shortcut and do a Google search for "companies with moats" but there are a few problems with that.

1. The moat you read about is not really that wide or it never existed.
2. The moat once existed but is now gone.
3. The articles you find may be poorly written, inaccurate, or biased. You can find better facts yourself.

But if you use caution and remain critical, it can't hurt to try a Google search for companies with moats; you may uncover some useful information.

Reading annual reports, watching videos where the CEO or other leaders are talking about their business will help you learn as much as you can about a company. You want to get a feel for whether a company is dominating its niche. Sometime you might hear a competitor refer to them as the ones to beat. Or maybe you'll notice that when they release a new product, everyone wants to buy them.

For example, I keep noticing people who seem to have good style sense wearing Nike sneakers. Now I have known the brand since I was a kid, and I still buy shirts or hats or sneakers from time to time, but I was not aware of how cutting edge the brand is today. There is a whole world of fashion, design, and an app called SNKRS[15], which Nike has been refining to connect super fans with desirable pairs of sneakers.[16]

I assure you that I'm not part of the fashion elite, but I do take note that Nike is not playing it safe and just making sneakers for sports. They spend a lot on advertising, and they push their sneakers and clothing into the spotlight as high fashion. I know it's working because on a recent flight the guy sitting next to me sporting bright white Nike high tops told me that he buys newly released rare Nike sneakers and then sells them on eBay for hundreds of dollars more than he paid.[17] It's his side hustle while going to school, and it seemed to be working for him. The fact that a huge company like Nike has created such demand for its products and kept them from being perceived as a cheap product or a commodity suggests it has a strong moat. Adidas, Under Armour, and Puma have many followers, but not the moat that Nike possesses.

Nike's North American position is about as dominant as they come. In 2016, it held 50.8 per cent of the U.S. retail brand footwear market, while Adidas improved its share to 7.4 per cent.[18]

The more you can read, watch videos, and learn about a company the better off you'll be forming an expert opinion about whether a moat exists.

To help you find companies with wide moats, I'll share with you a brief list of companies that I believe have wide moats.

All companies loosely fall into three categories: those that don't possess a moat, those with narrow moats, and those with wide moats. To keep things simple, I'm only interested in the latter.

Companies with moats I understand:[19,20]
  Adobe
  Alphabet
  Amazon
  Apple
  Berkshire Hathaway
  Costco
  Disney
  Intuitive Surgical
  McDonald's

Microsoft
Nike
Starbucks
Waters

I believe all of these companies are, to some extent, resistant to competition and will continue to widen their moats.

I'll briefly describe Adobe and Intuitive Surgical, two wide-moat businesses that I don't own as of this writing.

Adobe

I know this company through my experience as a photographer. Adobe (ADBE) develops Photoshop, a powerful photo-editing software program. Adobe also develops other software programs that photographers, graphic designers, and illustrators use: Lightroom, Illustrator, InDesign. In addition, Adobe develops Premiere, a professional video editing program. All of these products are considered powerful tools used by professionals.

Because Adobe is usually the first choice of image-editing software used by creative professionals, Adobe essentially has a monopoly in creative software. There are many second and third-tier software options available, but none of them pose a serious threat to Adobe's dominance. One of the main reasons why Adobe's market wide moat is so secure is due to the high switching cost.

Any photographer, graphic designer, animator, illustrator, or filmmaker who wants to switch to other software and solution has to relearn a new interface. It can take several years to learn how to use new software, especially if that new software is difficult to master. Alternative software options may offer features that don't even stack up compared to Adobe's or it may not be compatible with their operating system. With so many unknown variables providing high switching costs, most professionals will likely stick to software they already understand. This stickiness provides Adobe with a wide moat to protect their customers from any competitor's offers.

Adobe provides terrific tools to artists, photographers, designers, marketing professionals, and filmmakers and they offer them as subscriptions, which encourages recurring monthly streams of income.

The wide range of people who use these products, the reality that few other products barely come close to competing, and the ease of use of the cloud-based subscription model all combine to provide a wide moat. Any new product innovations, such as Adobe's new foray into stock photography with Adobe Stock will only serve to widen the company's moat.

Intuitive Surgical

I first learned about this company many years ago. I was photographing heart surgery at the time, and one of the surgeons I worked with mentioned the "da Vinci" robotic-assisted surgical system developed by Intuitive Surgical (ISRG). This company has a moat because it has a large base of installed robotic machines.

As of March 31, 2018, Intuitive Surgical had 4,528 da Vinci surgical systems installed in hospitals and universities around the world. If you added all of its competitors together it would not even come close to Intuitive Surgical's installed base of robotic operating machines.

Intuitive Surgical has also spent several years training surgical staff on how to operate its machines, which range in price from $0.5 million to $2.5 million. This familiarity within the medical community is valuable because its users are unlikely to search beyond the da Vinci system for a long time to come. A competitor would have to start from scratch in developing not only the machines, but earning trust in the healthcare industry, which is tightly regulated and very resistant to change. In addition, the surgical staff who are already familiar with the da Vinci machines would have to learn how to use a totally new system. This learning curve provides a barrier to entry for any newcomer, which further widens Intuitive Surgical's moat.

The company also has excellent operating margins. The company not only makes money selling its expensive operating machines. In reality, these high-tech machines cost a lot to build, and when they're sold they yield low profit margins. Most of Intuitive Surgical's margins come from selling the instruments used with each procedure, and also from fixing the machines when they need service. The instrument and service categories will likely grow over time.

Because they are the only major robotic-assisted surgery machines in the world, and they help doctors do procedures with low risk of complication, Intuitive Surgical is a wide-moat business.

Intuitive Surgical is already used frequently in urology and gynecology surgeries, and it has lots of room to grow in colorectal, cardiovascular, and general soft tissue surgical procedures. This lollapalooza of surgeries that its systems can address in a world that embraces technology as a way to save money and reduce surgical errors will provide a long runway and resistance from competition for years to come.

Some moats are hard to identify

I like the CVS pharmacy chain. I first saw them in my hometown of Newton, Massachusetts and have watched as they expanded across the country. I think they would probably be a good company to own, but I don't think they have a wide moat. I know they have competition from Walgreens, Costco, and Rite Aid and I imagine it's hard to have a wide moat in a commodity-type business of selling medications and retail pharmacy items.

It's too hard to know if CVS has a moat, so I just pass on making any decision about that stock. I simply don't know enough about the business, and if it will continue to be the dominant player in the pharmacy sector. Here is one main reason I'd be afraid of owning CVS for the long term: Amazon purchased PillPack Inc, a full service online pharmacy[21]. Its offer is that it helps users skip the pharmacy lines because the company sorts and delivers medication right to your door. If Amazon bought PillPack then it's definitely thinking of entering the online pharmacy business. If they did then stores like CVS and Walgreens would be much less valuable as their store traffic would drop. Much of a pharmacy's profit comes from snacks and other retail items sold to customers who visit a pharmacy to pick up prescriptions. If Amazon enters that market segment I would consider a large investment in a drugstore a precarious one at best.

How do you find moats?

What's the best way to find moats? Well, I'd hate to burst your bubble, but there is no shortcut. You have to learn about the company and do your homework. With time and reading you will start to figure out if a company had a moat or if it's just one of many companies fighting for scraps in an extremely competitive arena.

One thing I should mention is that the resources that I'll show you to help you find moats contain financial information; dollar amounts and terminology like cash flow, revenue, income. These are basic accounting terms, and even if you haven't taken an accounting course you can find their definitions through a quick search.

It might seem daunting at first, but don't expect to understand everything right away. Learn a little at a time, and over the course of a few weeks, months, and years, your knowledge will compound.

The two resources I think will help you find businesses with moats are Value Line and Morningstar Premium, which are described in the previous chapter. I have access to databases of both services through my local library in Seattle. You may want to check if your own library provides similar access. If they don't you can subscribe to both services on a monthly or annual basis.

Value Line provides an in-depth analysis of individual companies, and in my opinion they provide the most useful set of numbers for stocks in America. You can use their guides as a quick "thumbnail" of any company you're interested in to quickly measure one business against another. Their guides give you the best way to quickly figure out which companies are worth diving in and examining deeper, and which are best to just say "no" to and move on. You'll find Warren Buffett and Charlie Munger's opinions on Value Line below.

Morningstar's premium service provides analyst commentary, financial information, and moat ratings: none, narrow, wide. You can filter all companies in their database to filter for moats. Morningstar is a good way to get a quick idea of the absence or presence of moats.

Morningstar's database does not provide the moat ratings for all companies, and there is no guarantee that these moat ratings are accurate. I consider them a good starting point and, along with other data, it will help you form a clear picture of the company to decide if it makes sense as an investment.

Moats are a powerful investing filter because it helps you rule out many companies. You can just discard all kinds of businesses that are impermanent or fragile and focus on those durable companies that will likely dominate for years to come. If you are decisive on an outstanding wide-moat company you don't have to make many decisions. You can just sit back.

NINE

HOW TO READ AN ANNUAL REPORT

LEARNING to read an annual report is a lot like learning to read a foreign language. The language of business is accounting, so if you've taken an accounting class you'll have an easy time reading financial documents.

Well, you can buy stock in a company without reading the annual report. You'll still own the stock, but your successes or failures will seem random because you won't have an intimate understanding of what the hell is going on in the company. The company's management uses the annual report, which is full of numbers, to explain everything about its business during the past year and plans for the future.

It's no surprise why most annual reports get thrown right into the recycle bin. The text and colorful digital photos on glossy paper are easy to understand, but they teach you nothing. The numbers in the back are nearly impossible to understand, and they're supposed to be the most important part.

So what's an investor to do? Well, I want to show you how to get something out of an annual report in a few minutes, and that's all the time you need to spend with one. I'm going to lead you through an annual report and show you how exactly what you need to know to make sense of it.

Let's take a look at NVIDIA Corporation's 2018 Annual Report as the example. If you want to download it and follow along it just do a quick Internet search, download it, and follow along.

The annual report to shareholders

The annual report to shareholders is a small book (really a pamphlet), and it often has a glossy cover, photos, and includes a letter to shareholders from the CEO. The annual report is the company's one chance to communicate with shareholders during the year, and they put time and energy into making the report accurately express the financial condition of the company and what happened over the past year. Let's start by looking at the NVIDIA Corporation annual report.

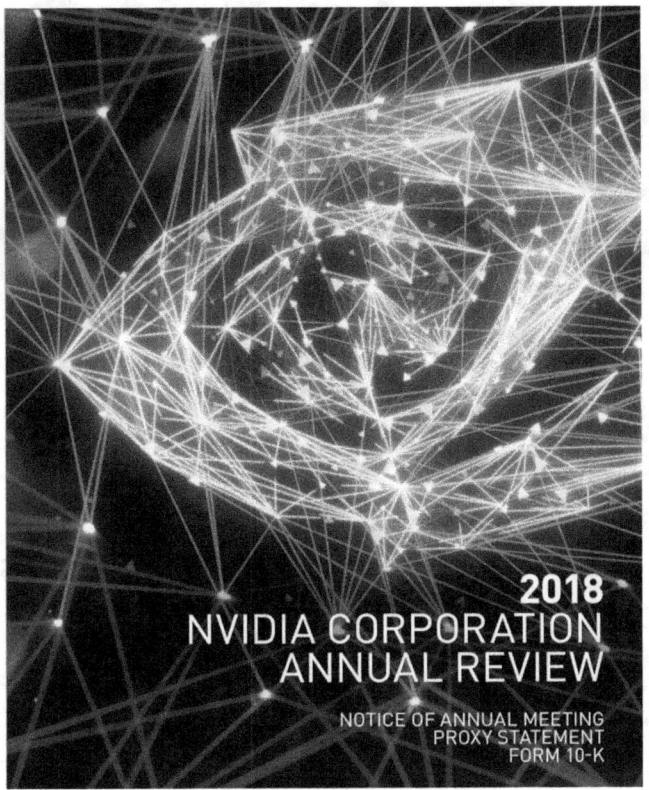

Just to give you a little background, NVIDIA started out with a focus on PC graphics, and then invented the graphics processing unit, or GPU, to solve some of the most complex problems in computer science. In recent years they have extended their focus to artificial intelligence, or AI.

If you take a look at the 2018 NVIDIA annual report, you'll see it has a beautiful color image on the cover, and some inside are some pretty color pictures of scientists using GPU computing to see gravitational waves for the first time in human history, a photo taken by NVIDIA Ansel, a powerful in-game camera that lets users take photos of their games, and someone driving "hands-free" in a car that uses NVIDIA DRIVE PX Pegasus supercomputer the size of a license plate.

I breeze past all those photos and turn directly to the Consolidated Balance Sheet printed on page 43 of the report (see chart below). The balance sheet lists the assets and then the liabilities. Those are the two most important items to me and I'll show you why. First, let me tell you which numbers matter.

NVIDIA CORPORATION AND SUBSIDIARIES
CONSOLIDATED BALANCE SHEETS
(In millions, except par value)

	January 28, 2018	January 29, 2017
ASSETS		
Current assets:		
Cash and cash equivalents	$ 4,002	$ 1,766
Marketable securities	3,106	5,032
Accounts receivable, less allowances of $13 as of January 28, 2018 and January 29, 2017	1,265	826
Inventories	796	794
Prepaid expenses and other current assets	86	118
Total current assets	9,255	8,536
Property and equipment, net	997	521
Goodwill	618	618
Intangible assets, net	52	104
Other assets	319	62
Total assets	$ 11,241	$ 9,841
LIABILITIES, CONVERTIBLE DEBT CONVERSION OBLIGATION AND SHAREHOLDERS' EQUITY		
Current liabilities:		
Accounts payable	$ 596	$ 485
Accrued and other current liabilities	542	507
Convertible short-term debt	15	796
Total current liabilities	1,153	1,788
Long-term debt	1,985	1,983
Other long-term liabilities	632	277
Total liabilities	3,770	4,048
Commitments and contingencies - see Note 12		
Convertible debt conversion obligation	—	31
Shareholders' equity:		
Preferred stock, $.001 par value; 2 shares authorized; none issued	—	—
Common stock, $.001 par value; 2,000 shares authorized; 932 shares issued and 606 outstanding as of January 28, 2018; 868 shares issued and 585 outstanding as of January 29, 2017	1	1
Additional paid-in capital	5,351	4,708
Treasury stock, at cost (326 shares in 2018 and 283 shares in 2017)	(6,650)	(5,039)
Accumulated other comprehensive loss	(18)	(16)
Retained earnings	8,787	6,108
Total shareholders' equity	7,471	5,762
Total liabilities, convertible debt conversion obligation and shareholders' equity	$ 11,241	$ 9,841

This is the NVIDIA balance sheet. You can find and peruse this in less than a minute to see if a company whose stock you're thinking of buying has an improving or deteriorating balance sheet.

In the top column titled Current Assets, I notice that the company has $4.002 billion in cash and cash equivalents, plus $3.106 billion in marketable securities. Adding these two items together, I get the company's current overall cash position, which I round off to $7.11 billion. Comparing the 2017 cash to the 2018 cash in the right-hand column, I see that NVIDIA is socking away more and more cash. This is a sure sign of prosperity.

Then I go to the other half of the balance sheet, down to the entry that says "long-term debt." Here I see that the 2018 long-term debt is $1.985 billion, virtually unchanged from last year. Ultimately I like to see the long-term debt reduced, but it's okay if it remains the same; you just don't want it to increase too much.

Debt reduction is another sign of prosperity. When cash increases relative to debt, it's an improving balance sheet. When it's the other way around, it's a deteriorating balance sheet.

Subtracting the long-term debt from cash, I arrive at $5.12 billion, NVIDIA's "net cash" position. The cash and cash equivalents alone exceed the debt by $5.12 billion. When cash exceeds debt it's very favorable. No matter what happens, NVIDIA isn't about to go out of business.

You may have noticed NVIDIA's short-term debt of $15 million. I ignore short-term debt in my calculations. The purists can fret all they want about this, but why make things complicated? I assume that the company's other assets (inventories, etc.) are worth enough to cover the short-term debt, and I keep moving.

As often as not, it turns out that long-term debt exceeds cash, the cash has been shrinking and debt has been growing, and the company is in weak financial shape. That's a company you don't want to own. This exercise is just going to let you know if the company is weak or strong.

Next, I look at the first page of the 10-K and can see that the number of shares of NVIDIA common stock outstanding as of February 26, 2018 was 605 million.

Dividing the $5.12 billion in cash and cash equivalents by the 605 million shares outstanding, I conclude that there's $8.46 in net cash to go along with every share of NVIDIA. In some companies you may have a situation where the stock might be selling for $80 but there's $8.46 of cash to go along with every share. That means that the stock is actually cheaper — it's as thought the stock is trading closer to $81.50. With NVIDIA selling at $172.69[1] about 5% of the stock price is backed up by cash — money in the company to back up the shares. NVIDIA is not a deteriorating company that's saddled with debt. Having a lot of extra cash in the bank is always a good problem to have.

TEN

ANATOMY AND DISSECTION OF A 10-K

THE 10-K (or simply the "K[1]") is a packet of different financial reports that shows the financial condition of the company at year's end[2]. It describes the company's financial health, revenues, debts, and profits, and also risks to the business so investors can get a full-color picture of the company's financial condition during the past year[3].

Why read the 10-K?
You can travel to France and get by just fine without without speaking French. Sure, you can get away with speaking English most of the time with an occasional "bonjour," and "merci" thrown in, but your travels will be more rich and memorable if you speak French. We're not talking about being perfectly fluent, but having a basic conversation skills will make it so much easier to meet real Parisians and one day you'll find yourself with your new friends, sharing wine and a baguette along the banks of the Seine as the sun descends, or sharing a breakfast of coffee, croissants & fruit.
I know this can happen because when I was 27 I traveled through

Europe by train, going from Paris to Barcelona to Lisbon and then Geneva, sometimes in a sleeper car in a train and other times staying in youth hostels, in farm yards, and in apartments in the city. In many places I became friendly with people who didn't speak English *because I knew their language.*

Just as you'll develop a more intimate connection to a culture when you understand their language, you can understand a company on a deep level if you're *familiar with the language of business*: accounting.

If the previous chapter about how to read an annual report was just enough working with financial numbers then please feel free to skip this chapter — you won't miss anything, and you won't fail as an investor! This chapter does give you some extra tools to "drill down" into a company's financial reports to see all of the moving parts of the business, but you don't have to know these details to succeed. I invested for many years without knowing what a 10-K was, and I did fine. I just wish I'd known how to read one, and I never found a book that explained it clearly, so I decided to write this book for you.

So for those of you who would rather sit in rush hour traffic on a hot day with no AC than read a bunch of numbers, I totally understand that, and you are forgiven in advance for skipping this chapter! It will be here for you later if you feel like returning to it. However, if you're one of those people who likes to get granular and dissect things to see how everything works, I'm going to show you how to dig into the 10-K to gain an understanding that few mortals will ever have about the company. You will truly be an expert.

Just for perspective, who actually reads these financial documents? Well, Warren Buffett happens to enjoy reading annual reports[4] from cover to cover and he reads every footnote. I'm sure it comes as no surprise that he's also the greatest living investor.

Financial analysts who work for brokerage firms like Goldman Sachs read annual reports because their job is to recommend stocks to brokers and their customers[5]. The analysts who work for mutual funds, pension funds, and universities like Harvard or Yale recommend stocks for their portfolio managers to buy[6].

So, as you can see, the people who make stock decisions that have a lot riding on them want to understand every detail of a business so they can see a little further into the future about potential new positive developments, and also to try and steer clear of any potential disasters. As a regular "small" investor who is in all likelihood not managing billions of dollars, you are not required to do the same reading as the professionals. But what if you had access to the same top secret information? What would you do with these superpowers?

Let's dive in and learn how to read a 10-K.

The 10-K

The language of business is accounting, so if you've already taken an accounting course you'll be especially well-equipped to read a 10-K. Have no fear, however, because if you haven't taken an accounting class you can still pick apart and understand a 10-K, and I'll show you how. I have never taken accounting, and I had to learn everything on my own. It takes time and watching a lot of videos, but it's all possible. I'm going to break down a year's worth of learning about reading a 10-K in the following pages.

If you're considering buying stock in a company at the moment, then I encourage you to download its 10-K right now. It will only take a minute to find and download it...I promise, it's really easy. Just search for the company name followed by the words "annual report." Once you start reading through the annual report you'll arrive at the 10-K.

If you just want to start reading the 10-K, then just type in the company name and 10-K. For example, we will look at Microsoft's 10-K together, so to find that document I Googled "Microsoft 10-K" and it was the first result. Easy peasy.

I promise you that the 10-K is not hard to understand. I will show you how to follow and learn from it.

How to read the 10-K

Keep in mind that every business is different and that will dictate the way you should read their specific annual report. What might be important to look at for an apparel company like Nike might be different than a tech company like Apple or an entertainment company like Disney, so be prepared to put on a different "thinking cap" for the variety of companies out there.

You don't want to end up missing something crucial to making an investment decision because you paid close attention to only the details I outline in this chapter. Keep in mind this is meant to give you a good overview, but I want to encourage you to spend as much time on any part of the 10-K as you want. I don't want you to miss out on any details crucial to your investment decisions.

So with that, here is a full breakdown of how I like to look through a 10-K for the first time, what's important to focus on, and what can be skipped over to save time and not fall asleep from boredom.

Business Description

The first part of the 10-K provides a description of the business. It doesn't matter how much I think I know about the business at the start, I always approach it like a total newbie because I want new eyes and go in pretending I don't know anything about it yet. So I'll skim the cover page to make sure I know where the headquarters are located, how many shares of the company are outstanding, what the market capitalization is, and when the fiscal (business) year ends. It's all basic stuff, but it's a good habit to peruse the basic description before you continue.

Perusing the Microsoft 2018 10-K (you can download it if you want to follow along) I see that aggregate market value of the company's common stock was $650.1 billion[7] and there were

7,668,217,316 shares of common stock outstanding. Right away something struck me: the current market value of Microsoft's common stock in September 2019 is $1.04 trillion, so in a short period of time the company's market value has increased more than $350 million. That's something I wouldn't have noticed without reading the business description.

UNITED STATES
SECURITIES AND EXCHANGE COMMISSION
Washington, D.C. 20549

FORM 10-K

☒ ANNUAL REPORT PURSUANT TO SECTION 13 OR 15(d) OF THE SECURITIES EXCHANGE ACT OF 1934

For the Fiscal Year Ended June 30, 2018

OR

☐ TRANSITION REPORT PURSUANT TO SECTION 13 OR 15(d) OF THE SECURITIES EXCHANGE ACT OF 1934

For the Transition Period From   to

Commission File Number 001-37845

MICROSOFT CORPORATION

WASHINGTON	91-1144442
(STATE OF INCORPORATION)	(I.R.S. ID)

ONE MICROSOFT WAY, REDMOND, WASHINGTON 98052-6399
(425) 882-8080
www.microsoft.com/investor

Securities registered pursuant to Section 12(b) of the Act:

COMMON STOCK, $0.00000625 par value per share	NASDAQ

Securities registered pursuant to Section 12(g) of the Act:

NONE

Indicate by check mark if the registrant is a well-known seasoned issuer, as defined in Rule 405 of the Securities Act. Yes ☒ No ☐

Indicate by check mark if the registrant is not required to file reports pursuant to Section 13 or Section 15(d) of the Exchange Act. Yes ☐ No ☒

Indicate by check mark whether the registrant (1) has filed all reports required to be filed by Section 13 or 15(d) of the Securities Exchange Act of 1934 during the preceding 12 months (or for such shorter period that the registrant was required to file such reports), and (2) has been subject to such filing requirements for the past 90 days. Yes ☒ No ☐

Indicate by check mark whether the registrant has submitted electronically and posted on its corporate website, if any, every Interactive Data File required to be submitted and posted pursuant to Rule 405 of Regulation S-T (§232.405 of this chapter) during the preceding 12 months (or for such shorter period that the registrant was required to submit and post such files). Yes ☒ No ☐

Indicate by check mark if disclosure of delinquent filers pursuant to Item 405 of Regulation S-K (§229.405 of this chapter) is not contained herein, and will not be contained, to the best of registrant's knowledge, in definitive proxy or information statements incorporated by reference in Part III of this Form 10-K or any amendment to this Form 10-K. ☐

Indicate by check mark whether the registrant is a large accelerated filer, an accelerated filer, a non-accelerated filer, a smaller reporting company, or an emerging growth company. See the definitions of "large accelerated filer," "accelerated filer," "smaller reporting company," and "emerging growth company" in Rule 12b-2 of the Exchange Act.

Large accelerated filer ☒   Accelerated filer ☐

Non-accelerated filer ☐ (Do not check if a smaller reporting company)   Smaller reporting company ☐

Emerging growth company ☐

If an emerging growth company, indicate by check mark if the registrant has elected not to use the extended transition period for complying with any new or revised financial accounting standards provided pursuant to Section 13(a) of the Exchange Act. ☐

Indicate by check mark whether the registrant is a shell company (as defined in Rule 12b-2 of the Exchange Act). Yes ☐ No ☒

As of December 31, 2017, the aggregate market value of the registrant's common stock held by non-affiliates of the registrant was $650.1 billion based on the closing sale price as reported on the NASDAQ National Market System. As of July 31, 2018, there were 7,668,217,316 shares of common stock outstanding.

DOCUMENTS INCORPORATED BY REFERENCE

Portions of the definitive Proxy Statement to be delivered to shareholders in connection with the Annual Meeting of Shareholders to be held on November 28, 2018 are incorporated by reference into Part III.

The first page of the Microsoft 10-K. There you have it, this might actually be the first time you've seen one of these documents. If you're thinking of buying stock in a company, I highly recommend downloading the 10-K and reading through it. Don't be intimidated, it's an important step in becoming an expert about the company.

The business description is the first part of every 10-K. You can check out the history of the business and any changes in the company's business segments. I have not carefully trained accounting training, yet it says it right there plain as day: "We operate our business and report our financial performance using three segments: Productivity and Business Processes, Intelligent Cloud, and More Personal Computing. Our segments provide management with a comprehensive financial view of our key businesses."

BUSINESS

GENERAL

Embracing Our Future

Microsoft is a technology company whose mission is to empower every person and every organization on the planet to achieve more. We strive to create local opportunity, growth, and impact in every country around the world. Our platforms and tools help drive small business productivity, large business competitiveness, and public-sector efficiency. They also support new startups, improve educational and health outcomes, and empower human ingenuity.

We continue to transform our business to lead in the new era of the intelligent cloud and intelligent edge. We bring technology and products together into experiences and solutions that unlock value for our customers. In this next phase of innovation, computing is more powerful and ubiquitous from the cloud to the edge. Artificial intelligence ("AI") capabilities are rapidly advancing, fueled by data and knowledge of the world. Physical and virtual worlds are coming together to create richer experiences that understand the context surrounding people, the things they use, the places they go, and their activities and relationships. A person's experience with technology spans a multitude of devices and has become increasingly more natural and multi-sensory with voice, ink, and gaze interactions.

The first two paragraphs of Microsoft's business description. From the 2018 Microsoft 10-K which is a part of the 2018 Annual Report. You can find it here: https://www.microsoft.com/en-us/annualreports/ar2018/annualreport

So right there I can see that Microsoft uses three segments. The way a business perceives its moving parts is crucial to understanding what they think is most important to their future. Reading through the Microsoft 10-K I can see that building on the "Intelligent Cloud Platform" with Microsoft Azure, and innovating with AI are big parts of where the company sees its future opportunities.

Here is what I want to learn:

1. What is the heart of the business?

What is the company's main cash generator, *the heart of its business*? Most of the time this isn't going to be the same segment as what I'm looking for in #2, but it's very important to understand what the major cash generator is for the company. A company can't survive without its cash generator so it can develop high-growth areas, so determining the key risks are just as significant as determining the catalysts to the explosion of another segment. Let's take a look at Adobe, which is based in San Jose, California.

Here's how Adobe explains its business segments in the 2018 10-K[8]:

"*Our business is organized into three reportable segments: Digital Media, Digital Experience, and Publishing...*"

> The flagship of our Digital Media business is Adobe Creative Cloud—a subscription service that allows members to use Adobe's creative products integrated with cloud-delivered services across desktop, web and mobile devices. Creative Cloud members can download and access the latest versions of our creative products such as Photoshop, Illustrator, Premiere Pro, Lightroom CC, InDesign, Adobe XD and many more creative applications. To expand our reach and improve the way we serve the needs of our customers, we create different combinations of these services, including our launch of a mobile photography offering that has brought new customers into our franchise and grown the amount of our photography subscriptions. In addition, members can access built-in templates to jumpstart designs and step-by-step tutorials to sharpen skills and get up to speed quickly. Through Creative Cloud, members can access online services to sync, store, and share files across users' machines, access marketplace, social and community-based features within our Adobe Stock and Behance services, and create apps and websites, all at affordable subscription pricing for cost-sensitive customers.

If you read through the description of the company's business segments it's going to be fairly obvious where it makes most of its money. The first line of managements description says "The flagship of our Digital Media business is Adobe Creative Cloud — so that's their cash cow.

As you can see, management explains that "The flagship of our Digital Media business is Adobe Creative Cloud—a subscription service that allows members to use Adobe's creative products integrated with cloud-delivered services across desktop, web and mobile devices. Creative Cloud members can download and access the latest versions of our creative products such as Photoshop, Illustrator,

Premiere Pro, Lightroom CC, InDesign, Adobe XD and many more creative applications."

So, Creative Cloud is clearly the heart of Adobe's business, the cash cow, the way Adobe makes most of its money. Every company will likely have one core product, and your job is to figure out what it is, and any risks associated with it in the future.

It then goes on to explain a marketing segment called "Digital Experience" and also the "Publishing" segment, the former being a potential growth area, and the latter a legacy business — so it's clear that Adobe Creative Cloud is the heart of the business.

1. What is the major growth generator?

Often a company like Adobe has a cash cow like Creative Cloud that constantly generates fresh money, but what happens if growth slows for a monopoly product? Adobe can raise prices on Creative Cloud for so long, but what if new customer growth tapers off, and the only way to grow revenue is to raise prices? That's not a long-term growth strategy. I reading more of Adobe's 10-K I discover what I think must be Adobe's growth generator, or where they hope to explode their cash flow in the future: its called "Digital Experience."

In plain English, it looks to me like "Digital Experience" is Adobe's marketing segment. I got that from reading a block of text that explain the following. This is is in the very beginning of the Adobe 10-K:

"...businesses must determine how to best attract, engage, acquire and retain customers in a digital world where the reach and quality of experiences directly impact success. Delivering the best experience to a consumer at a given moment requires the right combination of data, insights and content. Executives are increasingly demanding solutions that optimize their consumers' experiences and deliver the greatest return on marketing and IT spend so they can demonstrate the business impact of their programs using objective metrics.

The description goes on to show that there is a new market (this suggests they are not yet well-established) and they plan to use data and analytics and artificial intelligence to drive growth in this segment. Keep in mind, this segment may work out well or it could be a failure. But as a possible investor, you are getting a much better picture of what's going on than someone who never flips through he 10-K.

"We believe there is a significant opportunity to address these challenges and help customers transform their businesses. The world's leading brands are increasingly steering their marketing, advertising, and development budgets toward digital experiences... Our Adobe Experience Cloud business targets this large and growing opportunity by providing comprehensive solutions that include analytics, targeting, advertising optimization, digital experience management, marketing automation and engagement, cross-channel campaign management, content management, asset management, audience management, premium video delivery, digital commerce enablement, order management, predictive intelligence and monetization."

So there you have it, I believe this is Adobe's "major growth generator" for the future. It's important that you understand that this represents potential future growth as distinct from the current "heart" of their business: Creative Cloud.

Sometimes management highlights their major growth segment, but sometimes you have to dig for it, and keep in mind that it might not exist. Why is it so important to have a growth area? Well, having a cash cow like Creative Cloud is terrific, but Adobe won't be a great future investment if the main segment is only growing 1% a year and you're planning on owning the stock for decades or more. You need to find catalysts that show how the company can innovate and grow.

When you're reading through segment information, there is detail on segment growth. If sales (as a percent of the company's revenue) have moved up from the teens to twenties or thirties recently, you're probably looking at the growth generator.

1. What are the big risks for the "heart" and "growth generator"?

To find out about risks to a company's current business and future success let's keep things fresh by taking a look at a new 10-K, this one for Illumina, which is based in San Diego, California. Illumina is the global leader in genetic sequencing.

Even though Illumina is the 800 pound gorilla in the gene sequencing market, I can already see that competition is a serious threat to their business. The early text in the 10-K explains that genetic sequencing is a leading-edge technology, and scientific techniques are constantly being invented. It's possible that a competitor could come up with DNA sequencing systems that are better than what Illumina currently develops. Here's how they put it:

Although we believe that our products and services provide significant advantages over products and services currently available from other sources, we expect continued intense competition. Our competitors offer products and services for sequencing, SNP genotyping, gene expression, and molecular diagnostics markets. They include companies such as Affymetrix, Inc., Agilent Technologies, Inc., BGI, Pacific Biosciences of California, Inc., QIAGEN N.V., Roche Holding AG., and Thermo Fisher Scientific, Inc., among others. Some of these companies have or will have substantially greater financial, technical, research, and other resources than we do, along with larger, more established marketing, sales, distribution, and service organizations. In addition, they may have greater name recognition than we do in the markets we address, and in some cases a larger installed base of systems. We expect new competitors to emerge and the intensity of competition to increase. To compete effectively, we must scale our organization and infrastructure appropriately and demonstrate that our products have superior throughput, cost, and accuracy.

So consider yourself warned! Illumina may be the market leader right now, but in five or 10 years a lot can change. Illumina *could* be a good long-term holding, but this does not look like a "buy-once-and-forget-about-it" kind of investment. This is the kind of info you might not know as a casual observer, but when you dig into the 10-K you start getting a better picture of possible risks.

As I continue reading I find Item 1A that lists risk factors to the business.

> **ITEM 1A.** *Risk Factors.*
>
> Our business is subject to various risks, including those described below. In addition to the other information included in this Form 10-K, the following issues could adversely affect our operating results or our stock price.
>
> *If we do not successfully manage the development, manufacturing, and launch of new products or services, including product transitions, our financial results could be adversely affected.*
>
> We face risks associated with launching new products and pre-announcing products and services when the products or services have not been fully developed or tested. In addition, we may experience difficulty in managing or forecasting customer reactions, purchasing decisions, or transition requirements or programs with respect to newly launched products (or products in development), which could adversely affect sales of our existing products. For instance, in January 2016 we announced an expansion to our sequencing instrument platforms, the MiniSeq system, and we previewed a new sequencing system currently under development that will deploy SBS chemistry on a semiconductor chip. If our products and services are not able to deliver the performance or results expected by our target markets or are not delivered on a timely basis, our reputation and credibility may suffer. If we encounter development challenges or discover errors in our products late in our development cycle, we may delay the product launch date. The expenses or losses associated with unsuccessful product development or launch activities or lack of market acceptance of our new products could adversely affect our business, financial condition, or results of operations.
>
> When we introduce or announce new or enhanced products, we face numerous risks relating to product transitions, including the inability to accurately forecast demand (including with respect to our existing products), manage excess and obsolete inventories, address new or higher product cost structures, and manage different sales and support requirements due to the type or complexity of the new or enhanced products. Announcements of currently planned or other new products may cause customers to defer or stop purchasing our products until new products become available. Our failure to effectively manage product transitions or introductions could adversely affect our business, financial condition, or results of operations.

You can easily find the risk factors to the heart of the business and the major growth generator by reading through. Companies are very detailed in explaining all of the things that can go wrong.

This screenshot only the *start* of a long list of risk factors. As a potential investor you should be aware of them. I have listed the first four items below. If you want to read the entire list, you can find it in the Illumina 10-K[9].

- If we do not successfully manage the development, manufacturing, and launch of new products or services, including product transitions, our financial results could be adversely affected.
- Our success depends upon the continued emergence and

growth of markets for analysis of genetic variation and biological function.
- We face intense competition, which could render our products obsolete, result in significant price reductions, or substantially limit the volume of products that we sell.
- Our continued growth is dependent on continuously developing and commercializing new products.

Also, the Illumina 10-K has a cool picture and "Genetics Primer[10]" with some background information about genes, nucleotide bases, gene expression, messenger RNA (mRNA) and protein synthesis. Come for the financial statements, stay for the biology lesson! There are some diagrams and clear explanations, so if you want to brush up on your biology education you can get a nice refresher course for free.

Keep in mind...this might seem like a lot of work, but it you want to do better than the average investor you're going to have to put in extra work. The best way to get what you want in life is to deserve it, and you're well on your way if you're willing to spend several hours of your life understanding a company before you invest.

Some business risks are the same for every company so you can just skim that part, but company-specific risks like the ones described above for Illumina can disclose important information you might not find anywhere else. Remember, you're an investigative reporter trying to turn over every stone, follow every lead, and learn as much as you can about a business. You want to find vulnerabilities, or things that could seriously hurt the company. A company where conditions have to be perfect may run into serious problems if anything unexpected happens. Compare this to a company that has a solid, dependable customer base and regular stream of income plus some new areas of growth.

Management will usually outline key risks in the 10-K, and that will be a good starting point to figure out what you need to investigate further after you're done reading. Watch some videos, read articles about the company, keep looking and learning. It's actually a lot of fun, and you will feel good becoming an expert having so much understanding about a company you once barely understood.

Properties

You can skim through this part, no big deal here because there are no big surprises. It's just a list of offices, warehouses, distribution centers, administrative offices, etc.

Commitments/Contingencies

This is where you'd find out if the company is involved in any litigation. This is not particularly important for many companies, but sometimes it's linked with the business risks section. If you're looking at an oil company then management might highlight a certain lawsuit related to a spill, and if it's a tobacco company they may discuss litigation related to smoking. You just want to make sure there are no lawsuits that could devastate the company.

ITEM 5. Market For Equity

This is really basic stuff, and if you're looking at the stock you already know the range that the stock has been trading at recently. If the company pays a dividend it's listed in this section. If the company has been buying back its own shares this will also be listed here.

ITEM 6. Selected Financial Data

This is the first time you'll see the actual financial numbers that describe the performance of the business. It shows the financial highlights and lets you quickly see if the revenues are increasing or decreasing, it shows you the growth trends on important line items between the current and previous year on a number of specific line items, and gives you a bird's eye view of profit margins at the highest level.

I don't spend a lot of time on this section, but I think it makes sense to look it over to make sure nothing particularly horrible jumps out at you has happened like a huge one-time charge, a revenue shortfall, or a year where everything just sucked like an airplane toilet.

ITEM 7. Management's Discussion and Analysis

Management's discussion, along with the footnotes to the financial statements themselves, are where the rubber meets the road when it comes to figuring out what's really happening with a business. I'll read this over and take notes and I recommend you do too. The earlier parts were a warm-up for this part, which is often referred to as MD&A.

Get a nice cup / mug / carafe of coffee and some chocolate chip cookies or peanut brittle to take your time reading through this part. This is where the CEO and their management team discuss in plain terms what happened during the fiscal year. This is where they talk about successes, failures, and any big and /or cool projects they have in the works.

Highlights from fiscal year 2018 compared with fiscal year 2017 included:

- Commercial cloud revenue, which primarily comprises Microsoft Office 365 commercial, Microsoft Azure, Microsoft Dynamics 365, and other cloud properties, increased 56% to $23.2 billion.
- Office Commercial revenue increased 11%, driven by Office 365 commercial revenue growth of 41%.
- Office Consumer revenue increased 11% and Office 365 consumer subscribers increased to 31.4 million.
- LinkedIn contributed revenue of $5.3 billion, driven by strong momentum across all business lines.
- Dynamics revenue increased 13%, driven by Dynamics 365 revenue growth of 65%.
- Server products and cloud services revenue increased 21%, driven by Azure revenue growth of 91%.
- Enterprise Services revenue increased 5%.
- Windows original equipment manufacturer licensing ("Windows OEM") revenue increased 5%, driven by OEM Pro revenue growth of 11%.
- Windows Commercial revenue increased 12%, driven by an increased volume of multi-year agreements.
- Gaming revenue increased 14%, driven by Xbox software and services revenue growth of 20%, mainly from third-party title strength.
- Microsoft Surface revenue increased 16%, driven by a higher mix of premium devices and an increase in volumes sold, due to the latest editions of Surface.
- Search advertising revenue, excluding traffic acquisition costs, increased 16%, driven by higher revenue per search and search volume.

Highlights from Management's Discussion and Analysis in the 2018 Microsoft 10-K.

Just glancing at the highlights above, it's clear that Microsoft had a stellar year, with commercial cloud revenue, which includes

Microsoft Azure, increasing 56% to $23.2 billion. That's one hell of an increase.

Try to figure out what the important data is that the management team uses to assess performance, and accounting that you don't understand, and try to figure out how much cash the business has and whether it's wasting or losing money.

Earlier I mentioned how you want to think of yourself as an investigative reporter doing a story about the company. Well, as you read through this section just jot down any items that management explains that aren't clear to you, so you can ask "follow-up" questions to get clarification. This section will either leave you feeling unsettled or scared to invest in the company, or maybe it will make you feel confident that you understand the company's current trajectory and and have confidence on their future prospects.

ITEM 8. Financial Statements and Notes to Financial Statements

If you're just starting out in investing then you've done really well to make it this far into a description of the 10-K. As you've figured out, this is high-level fluent discussion of all aspects of the business. I don't expect you to immediately have the skills of an accountant or financial analyst, but my hope is that you won't be scared of flipping through the 10-K and getting a lay of the land.

I spent many years not even taking a look beyond the letter from the CEO because everything else was in a foreign language. I simply didn't know what any of the numbers meant.

I think that you can be an outstanding investor without spending all of your life immersed in financial statements and 10-Ks. If that's all it took to get rich then every financial analyst would have a yacht and live the easy life instead of battling it out on conference calls to try and figure out if a company will beat earnings by a nickel or fall short. Remember what Charlie Munger said, "Most people calculate too much and think too little."

You can get so immersed in these 10-Ks and other numbers that you don't really understand what's going on. I think it makes a lot of sense to understand a company and visit the 10-K to fill in any gaps in your understanding rather than to try and figure out a company from it's financial statements because while they give you a strong sense of the company's financial health they don't always grasp where the company is going. That's something you can't always read about, it's something you need to piece together on your own — and the financial statements can help you find your way along the path, but they're not a complete treasure map.

If you are obsessive about tracking financial data you can go line item by line item through the financial statement to see if everything syncs up to what you read about in the Management's Discussion and Analysis (above).

The most important part of this section for you to examine (wearing your investigative reporter hat) is the Notes to the Financial Statements. This can seem like the longest and most detailed section, and it will give you answers to any investigative reporters question that you might have. Any remaining questions you will still need to answer, and you can Google for the answers, or even call the company's investor relations line and ask them to explain anything that doesn't make sense to you.

Follow-Up

After finishing up reading all the important parts of the 10-K you will be quite an expert on the financial side of the company. This will put you far ahead of most investors in the company who never took the time.

You may, hopefully you have some questions left over. Those questions can probably be answered with some online searches, but if you can't find what you need, just search for the company's name and "investor relations phone" and give them a call. There is a department at every company that handles calls from shareholders, analysts, journalists, and everyone else who wants information about the company. Give them a call and ask your question, just like a tenacious reporter working on deadline!

I know I've gone into detail here, but I always knew you could skim this chapter if necessary. I simply have never found a book or video out there that went through the 10-K and told me what to skim and where to focus my energy. My hope is that you now are no longer scared to at least take a look at this document, and if you've taken away one or three pieces of useful info then my job will have been a success. Like I said, even knowing what a 10-K is and how to flip through and read it will put you way ahead of most casual investors.

Think like an investigative reporter

Also, just to give you a visual of how to think of this process: Imagine yourself as an investigative reporter, and you've decided to do an in-depth article about a company. You want to be tough, but fair in your reporting, but you will have to dig for information, become an expert, and even talk to real-life people — either customers, or vendors, suppliers, or the company leaders. I am not saying that you actually have to call up and speak to investor relations, or write to the CEO, but if you were writing an article about a company you certainly would do that. I have personally written to the CEOs of three companies I've invested in, and I've received responses — in one case a typed letter in the mail, and in two others people at the company got in touch with me via email. My point is that I'm not sitting around just googling stuff. I get involved because my money is involved, and I truly believe that asking good questions and paying attention to the answers can put you in a whole different league as an investor.

I'm pretty sure that none, or very few of the people I know have written to a CEO. In fact, only one person I know wrote to a CEO and he never got an answer. I think it was because in his case the question (or suggestion) wasn't useful or relevant. If you write to someone and you have some crazy agenda you can't expect a reply. It would be like you replying to spam email offering to answer some crazy scammers' request.

Back to reality: I imagine most people in the United States has access to paper, a pen, a stamp and an envelope, and can write a thoughtful letter. The same could be said of writing an email to ask a question. I think the reason most people don't do this is that it requires coming up with a question, and believing the answer to that question is something you care about, and writing that question in a way that makes the recipient think it's worth their time to respond. Easy and quick to do in five minutes? No. Could it be done in one hour? Yes, I've done it. It can be done.

So the people who truly pull ahead in the world of investing spend the time to think deeply, form questions, and ask those questions of others to deepen their understanding. I can't tell you what should interest you, and what the questions are that you may have about some company that fascinates you.

I believe that reading the annual report and the 10-K will make your curious and perhaps leave you asking some questions. And as you search for the answers you will learn more and more and increase your expertise and fluency with all matters relating to the company, which in turn will make you a better investor.

ELEVEN

PUTTING IT ALL TOGETHER

WE WILL NOW USE the eight-step filtering process with a real stock. When choosing the stock we'd look at I wanted to keep things exciting and timely, so I'm picking a stock of a relatively new company that had its initial public offering (IPO) in 2019. While it has been in the financial press lately because its stock has been going up like crazy, the company is not well-known worldwide and there's a chance you haven't yet heard of it.

I think the most exciting part of investing is learning about new businesses and what they're all about. I never know what kind of product or service they specialize in, or who's in charge of the business. It's a little bit like learning a new story, and each new piece of information helps you draw the outline, and fill in the details and color as you progress. Before long you'll have a complete picture.

To keep things fresh I'd like to look at stock that most people don't already know about, so we haven't formed an opinion about it. It's a new company that I just learned about a couple days ago.

Taking a chance on startups

Many of the stocks I've mentioned in this book are already established names. In order to fit through all of the filters in The TITANIUM Technique a business must be powerful, innovative, and resistant to competition.

But I've noticed that there's a problem with that kind of investing, and it's that you're only looking at big, well-established companies. Let's face it, by the time the company is a massive fortress with a moat around it to keep out the competition, everyone else has noticed the company too. It's already enormous and it's probably already finished it's fast growth phase.

For example, Starbucks was a fast growing company about 20 years ago, and this rapid growth continued until recently. Now, while still growing, it's so large that it's hard to keep growing at the same rate. This is the same for any established company; the larger you get, the harder it is to double or quadruple in size.

Example of a new company: Zoom Video Communications

I discovered a successful business the other day and I'm digging to find out as much as I can about Zoom Video Conferencing (ZM) as a potential investment. It's rare I find a business like Zoom where I'm impressed with the product and also see a CEO like Eric Yuan who exhibits talent and integrity.

How I learned about Zoom

I learned about Zoom on YouTube. I was originally watching a video about fast growing companies who had recently had IPOs, and this one jumped out at me because it was profitable. It really doesn't matter which way you prefer to absorb information, your goal is to become an expert on the company, and the only way to do that is total immersion. Think of the time you spend reading a favorite book, or playing a favorite video game. You need to dedicate some serious time to learning.

The important thing is to soak up lots of new information. You want to find as many new things about the company that resonate with you that you didn't know about before. Keep asking questions about the company. Could it be the next big thing?

All great businesses were were once unknown. Amazon seemed like an online bookstore when it began, and any company in its first few years is experimenting, trying to figure things out, and there are no guarantees of success. During their early days, businesses are like baby chicks in an incubator, sensitive to outside forces, a bit delicate and dependent on good conditions for lift-off. Nobody really understands how they will mature yet when they're still all warm and fluffy.

Investing in these hot start-ups will definitely not be boring, and there are more risks than investing in established companies like Apple, Costco, McDonald's or Proctor & Gamble, but if you remember back to Chapter 5 we discussed "intelligent speculation" as a way to buy stock in a company you'd usually have to say "no" to because you don't have perfect understanding.

You will want to invest a smaller amount in a separate account if you're going to speculate, and don't invest any more than you're willing to lose. Also, spread your investments out over time so you don't invest everything at a high price, and you increase the chances you'll get to buy some shares if the market crashes.

"As difficult as it is rare"

Finding a profitable business run by a talented leader with integrity, and buying that stock at a sensible price is like the holy trinity of investing. It doesn't get much better than that!

Though getting those three things to line up may seem simple, in reality it's not. If you can find those three qualities just three times in your life you'll wind up rich before long. I don't count on those things happening, but I think you can put yourself in a position to win by at least giving it a try if you have the right temperament for it and are willing to put in the time to learn.

While finding a fast-growing, profitable company with great leadership is about as rare as finding a squirrel playing the saxophone, when you discover one company like this it will just jump out at you. That's exactly what happened to me yesterday while I came across Zoom.

It's both difficult and rare to find a terrific company for long-term investment. Finding a profitable business run by a leader with talent and integrity, and buying its stock at a density is the holy trinity of investing. It's as rare as finding a squirrel playing the saxophone.

As with many companies, I figure it's beyond what I'm capable of knowing well, and I move on. Or I learn a bit about the CEO and they don't impress me. Or maybe the company makes a product that I can't get that excited about, it's not my scene, I just click, flip, or swipe to the next thing.

But Zoom kept my interest through each filter; it was video conferencing, which I'm familiar with (and you probably are too) if you've done Skype, FaceTime, GoToMeeting, etc. I'm mainly familiar with one-to-one video calls, but businesses and teams often have conference calls and I don't imagine they're that much different: it's video, it's a call, it's over the Internet.

So I understand the basics, and I was immediately curious about the CEO, and I wondered if they also happened to be the founder, because as you'll recall from Chapter 3 on talent, I have noticed enormous winds at your back when the founder of the company is also the CEO (think about Jeff Bezos, Steve Jobs, etc). It turns out that the company's founder, Eric Yuan, is also the CEO.

The more I read about Yuan, the more impressed I was. I watched an interview with him on YouTube and he was just the kind of talented leader I've searched for when I look at a company. I was surprised, honestly, because most of the companies I look at I just say "no" and move on. I've bought one new stock in the past several years, so clearly it takes a lot for a new company to pass my filter: it has to be a better opportunity than my other stocks, and that's a high hurdle to jump over. If any new idea is less good, I just forget it, because why put money into my sixth best idea when I can invest more in one of my top five?

But Zoom seems interesting for a number of reasons, and I'm going to spell them out here, not because I know a ton about this company, but because I want you to see my process and how I use The TITANIUM system and the way I treat a company I'm considering.

I want you to see my method so you can use it yourself. Just as a reminder, you should never buy Zoom or any stock because I, or anyone owns it or talks about it. As I said, I just learned about the company yesterday, and I admit to just starting to learn about it. Yet we all have to start somewhere, and I can help you by showing you my approach.

Obsession about customers

Hearing Zoom's CEO Yuan speak reminds me of Amazon's Jeff Bezos. Though Zoom will have competition from Microsoft's Skype, Cisco's Webex, and possibly future competition from Google, Facebook and Amazon, Yuan doesn't seem concerned. He said that he's just trying to take care of customers and make them happy, and everything will be okay.

"I think the way for us…most of time, we do not spend it on looking at competitors, really spend time to care about the customers," Yuan said. "Really want to understand, what's the pain point from the customer's side. We want to be the first company to understand the customer's pain point, to come up with the solution, be the first one, to take care of customers. If we keep doing that customers will trust us. Ideally, you know, even our competitors do not understand the customers' pain point. Then I think we can make the customer happy, I think we'll be okay[1]."

It was not only the words, but the belief behind them that make me think Yuan is the real thing. Of course, I may be fooled and he may not be as successful as he hopes, but his obsession on putting the customer at the center of the business makes sense.

"Titanium Technique" filter for Zoom

1. Temperament - I'm excited about this company and want to buy the stock, but I'm holding off right now. Not jumping in, patience.
2. Identify - I identified this company as one that is different

from most I see for a number of reasons. First, it's a newly public company through the IPO and it's profitable. This is unlike Tesla, Uber, Lyft, Beyond Meat, and a bunch of companies with recent IPOs.

3. Talent - I believe Eric Yuan is extremely talented. Before starting Zoom he worked at Cisco's Webex video conferencing and was frustrated that the company did not work hard enough to make it useful to customers. So he left a six figure salary at Cisco to start his own company to obsess over customers and provide a better experience. That is Zoom Video Conferencing.

4. A sensible price - No. I don't believe Zoom's current stock price of $117.47 makes any sense. I've looked closely at this company, its stock price, and the 31.26B market capitalization[2] at the close of the market on March 3rd, 2020. I have a problem with the company's current stock price. This is a "white hot" tech stock and its popularity has resulted in a high share price. What's an investor to do? In a nutshell, I would never give advice on a specific investment, but I would personally not buy the stock anywhere near the current price. No company is worth an infinite price, and I would wait and see if market fluctuations drop this into the $80s or below. My estimate of the value of the entire business is about 15B and if I divide that amount by the 293M shares outstanding[3], I estimate each share is worth $51.19, which is far less than the current quoted price of $117.47.

5. "No" - I've said no to a lot of other companies I've seen, and this one passes on many levels. I say "no" to Zoom as a sensible investment based on the high price, but if I wanted to invest in a collection of speculative stocks I'd consider Zoom.

6. Invest - This factor doesn't refer specifically to this stock.

7. Understand - Yes, I have a good understanding of the business and what it's product is all about, which is to deliver an easy-to-use cloud-based video conferencing platform accessible on a smartphone, tablet, laptop or in a conference room that is simple to use.
8. Moat - Zoom has steep competition from other tech companies like Skype (owned by Microsoft), Google, and possible future offerings from Amazon.com and Facebook. There's no moat for this company, so you'd have to be flexible and realize that if you're going to invest in a startup they won't be resistant to competition.

You can see that Zoom doesn't pass every filter of "The TITANIUM Technique," but that's because it's expensive and because it's a relatively young company, it lacks a moat. If Zoom stock got much cheaper (due to a market crash, the company missing earnings estimates, or some other reason) it would become a more compelling value and I would definitely consider buying the stock.

A stock can be a really bad investment at a high price and a great investment at a lower price. I could be wrong about the pricing for Zoom, and obviously I have no crystal ball. Plenty of people think the current stock price makes sense right now. The stock could climb from here forever and I might miss the chance to ever buy the stock because I sat around sucking my thumb waiting for a cheaper price. I'm willing to take that chance, as I find it's usually better to have a bit more patience and wait for a lower price. If you pay too much and the stock goes down a lot, it might never recover to the high price you paid, or it could take years to reach that level again.

Take it from me, I have bought stock and seen the price drop about 25%-30% right after I bought it and just wished I had either (1) just bought a little bit (instead of a lot) or (2) waited until the stock got a lot cheaper *and then* buy a lot. Of course nobody rings a bell when it's time to buy so you never know for sure, but there are signs that stocks are priced too expensively, and I think for some tech stocks that time is now.

It's valuable lesson for you to see me run through the eight questions with Zoom and decide for yourself if it does or doesn't pass. Sometimes it's hard to be patient, to have money sitting in my brokerage account waiting to buy shares of Zoom. That doesn't mean it's a good to buy. In this case, time will tell, but I think I can do better than the current price.

Let me just explain what I mean. Zoom did not pass #4 (a sensible price) or #8 (moat) above. In the future, however, the price could get cheaper and that would make Zoom a better investment. The price you pay greatly influences your returns. If you pay too much for a stock it could take you a long time to break even after a decline, or you may never break even. You don't want to lose money, and one of the best ways to do that is to buy cheaply, and give yourself some wiggle room in case you weren't perfect in estimating the value.

The earlier chapter where we looked at price as separate from value applies here. The price for Zoom is super high, in my opinion, when you compare it to the intrinsic value of the company. It's like paying $10 for a pint of ice cream, or $5 for a donut.

I can't prove it, but I have a feeling that Zoom is way too expensive right now with a market cap[4] of $24.1 billion. I can't see why Zoom, a company that makes one software app, has such a high valuation.

Think about that: Amazon has the retail website, Amazon Prime, Amazon Web Services, Alexa, Amazon Streaming Video, and Music, and many other segments. It went public in 1997 and is one of the largest companies on the planet, and it's current stock market capitalization is $860 billion. Zoom is a new company with one product and the market says it's worth $24.1 billion. I think the market is giving this too high a stock price, and the market is wrong.

I think the stock could not only fall to the $70 range soon, I think it's possible Zoom's stock price could fall into the $60 range. It would still be the same awesome company, just a lot cheaper. So consider yourself warned about super popular tech IPOs selling above their intrinsic value. I will definitely wait before I even think about buying Zoom.

I think that stock investors have bid the price up prices of IPOs to insanely high levels. According to an article in Baron's, "the market is generally welcoming at the moment to IPOs of software firms and consumer-facing unicorns—privately held companies value at $1 billion or more—such as Pinterest, Lyft, and Uber[5].

Zoom went public in 2019 and sells one software program. I think Zoom's profitability stood out to investors who are accustomed to tech-IPOS by mostly money-losing companies like Dropbox, Lyft, Uber and Tesla) has caused investors pile in. What might be a great buy at a lower price can be a horrible investment at another. I think $82.63 is just too much to pay, but I think the company may have a bright future and would be a good investment at a lower price. I'm willing to wait.

How much cheaper would it have to get before I bought the stock? Here is how I think about it, in a very simple, back-of-the-envelope math. I first have to decide what I think the whole company is worth. As of this writing they employ about 2,000 people and are located mainly in San Jose, California. I imagine the intrinsic value of the company (what I would pay for the entire company today if I was paying in cash) at $10B, which is actually on the high end of my estimate. I'm just giving it a slightly higher estimate of intrinsic value based on the fact that I think their software is truly a level above all other video conferencing programs available, it's an emerging growth company and it's already profitable.

What is Zoom stock really worth?

The next question I ask is: how many shares are outstanding? According to Bloomberg, there are 293,000,000 shares outstanding as of October 31, 2019 [6].

Now, I simply divide my intrinsic value estimate by the total shares outstanding.

$15,000,000,000 ÷ 293,000,000 = $51.19 per share.

Keep in mind that companies often issue new shares as bonuses for executives, employees, etc., so that number can grow quickly. You must have an accurate share count otherwise the amount you want to pay per share will seem greater than you should actually be willing to pay.

So you can see the problem here: The current stock price as of this writing is $82.63 and there are 293,000,000 shares outstanding. If we do this easy math:

$117.47 x 293,000,000 = $34,418,710,000.00

...we can see that investors are valuing the company at about $34.42B. Take a step back and look at that picture. A hot tech stock that has produced one software product is given an enormous valuation by the market.

Remember, I estimate the company is worth $15B. The market says it's worth more than double that amount.

What to do now?

I wait. Most people have never heard about this company that produces one software application. As I mentioned earlier, either Amazon is cheap, or Zoom is very expensive, and I'm leaning toward the latter being true.

"Stocks I'd Avoid"

In his book *One Up on Wall Street*[7], Peter Lynch wrote, "If I could avoid a single stock, it would be the hottest stock in the hottest industry, the one that gets the most favorable publicity, the one that every investor hears about in the car pool or on the commuter train—and succumbing to the social pressure, often buys."

Now, I don't think Zoom is the hottest stock in the tech industry, but it could well be among the top 10 unicorn stocks, and from a pricing perspective it's definitely in that cohort. That doesn't mean it's a bad company, but I think it suffers from being considered a hot stock.

In the same book he also warns, "Beware the stock with the exciting name," and goes on to say that a boring name is much better than an exciting one. Lynch's reasoning is that "a dull name in a good company keeps early buyers away, a flashy name in a mediocre company attracts investors and gives them a false sense of security," he said.

"As long as it has "advanced," "leading," "micro," or something with an *x* in it...people will fall in love with it."

Well, I think Zoom is getting some buzz from having a *z* in its name, and it's surely attracting investors. In this case I just take Peter Lynch's words of caution — not to avoid this stock, but to be very careful not to overpay. If it got a lot cheaper — like 30%—50% cheaper than where it is today, then it might be a better investment. For now, though, be careful about the hot stocks. You can lose a lot of money when the share price drops suddenly.

Markets fluctuate, and there's a good chance that Zoom's market price could dip down below the $80 mark sometime soon. It's September and lots of things happen can happen during the fall and winter months to cause the stock market to plummet. Stocks of tech companies, especially fast-growing tech startups, can get whacked in a market downturn. They are especially vulnerable as investors flee "risky" stocks of smaller firms and get invested in larger companies considered to be "safe" bets. Of course this is merely emotional thinking based on short-term fears, and when investors are panicking and selling their stocks the wise investor is on the other end of those trades.

By the way, I think the right investing mindset is to realize that the stock market is not there to teach us anything. The recent $117.47 closing share price[8] is simply an offer: you can take advantage of that price or ignore it. The stock price is there to serve you, but it's not there to instruct you. If you learn nothing else in this book, just remember that last sentence; it's a great take-home lesson.

I believe the current Zoom stock price is artificially inflated and batshit crazy. Obviously, I were a Zoom investor[9] I would hope the price went up in the future. But as a potential buyer, I hope the price declines, and from these levels I think it probably will.

Be patient, and let the market serve you. You may be pleasantly surprised to see what happens. You may notice that for some unexpected reason the stock drops 5% in a day. It doesn't mean the company is going down the tubes. Just think of it as the stock going on sale. You don't have to act, but take note. Try to figure out if the stock price drop is the result of a serious event at the company, or if it's just a market fluctuation.

I think there's a chance Zoom will drop into the $80 range, and I think a patient investor might see it in the $50 range. I have no way to forecast the market or stocks, but I think right now the market is voting on Zoom with optimism, and in the next several months it could settle on a lower and more rational price for the shares.

I don't know if Zoom stock will ever hit the $51.19 per share price that I estimate the company is worth. With each passing month the company may get (or lose) customers, and it may make (or lose) money, and as its future prospects snap into sharper focus the market will re-assess the stock price. If Zoom continues to grow its revenues and remains profitable the intrinsic value of the company will increase. The stock market is totally unpredictable, and the stock price will probably bounce around a lot in the near future. In the short term, as Benjamin Graham said, the market is a voting machine (like a popularity contest where people get excited about shiny things) but in the long term, it's a weighing machine, making more rational assessments. Stocks of profitable tech startups are in fashion right now, but that doesn't mean you have to overpay. Be patient, and you might have the opportunity to buy a great stock a lower share price if you can just wait for it.

. . .

What Eric Yuan said - and why it adds to his trustworthiness

Zoom Video Communications' stock skyrocketed 72% in its trading debut, closing at $62 a share. "The price is too high," Eric Yuan said in an interview with Bloomberg TV on Thursday. "Today, wow, there's a big pop. It is out of our control. We can just go back to work.[10]"

I just want you to take a look at what he said, because it's the first time I've ever seen a CEO say his company's stock price is too high, and it may be the last time as well.

It's a sign of a CEO's integrity to say that because many CEOs just want the stock price to go up, and in their eyes it can never be too expensive. The higher it goes, the richer everyone gets. But Yuan, who instantly made $3.2B as a result of the white-hot IPO, was not trying to get the stock price higher so he could become even richer. He knows the company and he truly felt the stock price was too high.

Two take-aways are that at the time of the IPO — in April 2019 — Yuan thought that $62 a share was too high. So today's price of $117.47 in March 2020 is possibly too high because I don't see anything major that happened to make the company suddenly worth 100% more. Think about that: the CEO said the stock was too high at $62 a share, and in less than 1 year it doubled. That's useful information to keep you from paying too much. Just hearing what a CEO with integrity says gives you one more data point in deciding whether to buy stock now or wait for an opportunity to buy at a more sensible price.

I admire that Yuan had the guts to say that because he's saying there are more important things than the stock price going up. He said that the price pop was out of their control, but "We can just get back to work." That's the work ethic I want in a leader. Less concerned with the stock price and more focused on actions that will help the company survive.

. . .

Why are IPOs such a big deal?

One of the things that really jumped out at me was that this was one of the companies that had a successful IPO in 2019. There have been a slew of companies to go public recently, and this usually happens when the stock market climbing, money is flowing freely and investors are excited.

If you think about it, it makes sense for a private company to "go public" through an IPO when everybody is excited about stocks, because the IPO shares are essentially free to the company, and suddenly all investors — small individual investors and institutions — often pay higher and higher dollar amounts per share to own the stock. This is why the founders, insiders[11] and early investors in the company can get rich so quickly. Their shares, which previously had no value suddenly become worth $20, $30, $50, $80 or more instantly. For a founder or early investors who own millions of shares the IPO can instantly make them billionaires.

It makes sense for companies to wait for the "perfect time" to have an IPO because they want to maximize how much people will pay for their stock. It's good for you to keep this in mind because you're on the other side of that equation. You're being sold something (stock), and the more you pay the wealthier the company's investors and insiders become. This is not a bad thing, but I think you deserve to know why there is so much hype and excitement in the media, on CNBC, and online about a company's IPO. The worst thing for a company is for the IPO to go unnoticed, which is why you see these new companies ringing the opening bell at the stock exchange, why you see the CEO interviewed on financial programs, and why suddenly there are lots of news stories popping up everywhere about new IPO stocks you should buy now. Stay skeptical and don't be swayed by the hype. It could be a great idea or a horrible idea, but I have noticed that often stocks hit their highs during the IPO and the price generally goes down quite a bit in the months afterward. It's just an observation I've made, and your mileage may vary.

. . .

Warnings about buying after an IPO

There are two things I've noticed often happen right after an IPO.

1. The company's stock trades at insanely high prices for a while because everyone and their mother want to buy the stock. It could be a great company, but they pay too much and you don't have to participate. In the months or years after the IPO I have noticed that the price often dips quite a bit, and that presents you with a buying opportunity at a more reasonable price.
2. There is a time called the "IPO Lockup" when pre-IPO shareholders and company insiders are not able to sell large quantities of restricted stock. When that lockup period expires these shareholders and insiders can sell their stock for the first time.
3. In the Zoom Video Communications example above, the company's IPO was on April 18, 2019 and the IPO lockup will expire on October 15, 2019 (which has not arrived as of this writing). A potential investor in the stock might be better off waiting until this date has passed, because Zoom stock has returned more than 113% in less than six months since the IPO, and when the IPO lockup ends the stock price could drop a lot.

Why buy stock in small companies?

I think it's great to find businesses when they're small. If you can recognize a great company early on when they're small (and not overpay) you can make many times your money. The only problem is that everyone else wants to get rich too! It's not easy to discover great companies before everyone else.

If you dedicate yourself to finding great companies when they're little, that can make a lot of sense. For example, if you bought Facebook's IPO in 2012, you could have likely known at that time that the company would be a success because everyone and their network of family and friends were on Facebook. You just had to know that it was the dominant social media platform and growing rapidly, and you could have known enough to buy the stock — and this was *before* Facebook bought Instagram for $1B, and by 2019 Instagram is widely believed to be worth more than $100B[12]. When Google went public in 2004 everyone knew it was the search engine that just about everyone used.

Of course now it's obvious that those would have been great investments, but at the time I think you could have bought either company with a high degree of certainty that their businesses would do well. It's not always obvious how profitable these companies will be, but it did not take a genius to realize Google was going to be an enormous success (Google was already the dominant search engine) and get in early, you can get rich in the long term just buying and holding the stock.

Why not try to get 'em when they're small? A lot of people try to do exactly that, and it's a truly beguiling idea. If I had some great idea about a small company, I might actually focus on that company and any others I discovered.

So the question is, how do you get them small? Well, you have to look for them. You have to read a lot. I was watching videos about new technology companies and came across Zoom, otherwise I would never have heard of it.

So you need to read newspapers — the Wall Street Journal, The New York Times, The Financial Times, and any other publications that cover finance and investing.

Also, you might have to be flexible with your "TITANIUM Technique" filtering factors. A small business might not have a moat, which generally widens over time. But when a business is just starting out, it doesn't yet have a durable competitive advantage. So you might have to give a company a "pass" on not yet having a moat.

There is something in some of us that wants to be an early investor, take a chance, and get in early on a company *before* it becomes a huge success. We all want to find a diamond in the rough or stumble upon buried treasure. This desire to get lucky and is probably not going to disappear, but we don't have many situations in our modern world where we open an oyster and there's a pearl in it. Much of the luck around us comes after we've put in the hard work.

I think that's what's behind a lot of excitement about the stock market. I say excitement, meaning the gamblers and day traders and other people trying to get rich making a few big bets *today* instead of making a few long-term investments that come to fruition in 10 years and beyond.

Why do so many of us insist on trying so hard to beat the market and get rich quickly? It's probably because we're human beings, and even through we live in an advanced society we believe in magic. It's the triumph of hope over experience, the same hope you must possess to get married even when you realize 50% of marriages fail. If you were going skydiving and they told you half the parachutes won't open, would you jump[13]?

Well, hope and belief is a good thing, because it pushes us forward to try new things because we feel lucky and in some ways, this risk-taking can work out well if you work hard, learn a lot, and take some chances. In order for a marriage to work out, you first have to give it a chance, right?

So even though much of this book is dedicated to helping you make good decisions based on your understanding and patience, I believe if you're like me there might be something in you that still wants to take a chance on some stock that you're not sure about, and it's kind of an experiment. You want to open the freezer and eat huge scoops of mint chip ice cream. In the same way, taking a chance on that hot new company might not be such a great idea, but to be honest, you'll never experience the great investment if you wait until you're 100% sure. By then, it's too late, the company would already be a success and you'd be late to the party.

By the way, on the subject of living a long life, I recently saw a documentary on Richard Overton, the oldest living veteran, who's

109 years old, and he said the secret to his long life is (among other things) his daily serving of ice cream. Butter pecan is his flavor of choice. He offers this advice freely to those who would like to try it, along with a few other pieces of advice in a YouTube video[14].

Back to investing: what you really want to do is wait until you have about 70% of the information you wish you had before making a stock investment. You don't want to wait until you have every piece of information about the company before you buy, because if you wait too long you may never buy — all the while the stock price keeps climbing.

Remember that if you make a mistake and the company's story changes you can always sell your stock. Investing is imperfect because you can't know everything about a company and its future before you invest. So you have to experiment sometimes with your investment, and it's not experiment if you already know how it turns out. Also, you can always sell your stock later if you change your mind, so don't worry. If you really like a business, its leader, and it's growth prospects and the price seems fair, there is not harm in buying some shares.

If you get good at investing in smaller companies before they become well-known by everyone there's a chance your investment could grow to 10 or 20 times your original investment. This is not likely to happen with a large established company, because once a company has a market capitalization of 500B it's hard to double, and then double again. But if you're a small, fast-growing company it's much easier to double, triple, or grow to 10 times your original size quickly because you're starting small and it's easier to grow rapidly from a small size than once you're a huge company and growth starts to slow.

Also, I find that owning some shares — you don't have to own many — is a good way to follow a stock closely. When you have some "skin in the game[15]" you're more likely to keep up-to-date with what's going on with a company. If you don't own any stock then it's very theoretical and you may forget about it as it drifts from your mind.

TWELVE

HOPE STOCKS WILL GET CHEAP

YOU SHOULD ROOT for stock prices to go down, not up. I know it's counter-intuitive, but think about it this way, if you're buying something, wouldn't you rather pay less for it than more? It doesn't matter if you're talking about sneakers or a car or groceries, you should always want to buy stuff cheaply.

When stocks get cheaper, that's always good news for a long-term investor. There are very few times when you should be bold, and if you look at the history of the stock market — those times are exactly when it seems you should be most afraid and sell everything. But It's absolutely insanely crazy to sell stocks after they drop. Instead, you should say, "Today there's a phenomenal bargain and I'm buying."

Don't buy all your stock on the same day

The mistake that new investors always make is to go "all in" and buy a bunch of shares of a stock they like. Then, it never fails — the next day the stock price drops 5% or 7% or more. It almost seems the market knew you were overpaying for your stock, and after you bought, *then* the stock got cheap.

Here is one great tip I can offer: when you decide you want to buy stock, no matter how excited you are about the company, don't go "all in" on one day. Instead, buy shares in the stock over time. This is like free insurance to protect against you buying all your shares when they're trading at high prices.

By spreading your purchases out over time, you are lowering your average cost per share if markets happen to fall. For example, if you buy 10 shares today at $85 per share, and a few months later you buy 10 more shares, but the price has gone down to $65 per share, and a few months later you buy 10 more shares at a price of $50 per share, then your average cost is ($85 + $65 + $50) ÷ 3 = $66.67 per share. If you bought all of your shares at $85 then that would be your average cost. Buying in at different times offers some protection in case your first buy is at a high price.

If instead of prices going down they go up after your first purchase at $85, then it's true, you may have to buy more shares at higher prices, but at least you didn't overpay initially, you gave yourself some insurance to protect against paying too much for stock.

I actually did exactly this during the 2008 financial crisis. I had been buying shares of Leucadia National Corporation (LUK) in the $50 range before the financial crisis, and suddenly the stock dropped into the $35 range which I thought was really cheap, so I bought some more. Fortunately I didn't spend all my cash at the price even though it was so cheap. A few weeks later the price went down to $20 and I bought more. Then it went down to around $14 a share, and I bought yet more shares of the stock. The "take home lesson" here is that you might think a stock has become really cheap and it's a good time to spend all of your investible cash on it. Keep in mind that it may still get a lot cheaper, so keep some of your cash available in case the price continues to drop.

THIRTEEN

GET READY TO BUY STOCKS

I WOULD LIKE to put some cash to work right now, but I'm waiting. I like to buy stocks, and I've put together a list of five that I like. I hope you've been doing the same, either on a list you've written down or that you're keeping in mind. Yet, as much as I want to buy stocks I simply cannot right now. The prices for all stocks I like seem expensive to me. But I can be ready.

I'm ready to act decisively when, and only when, the right circumstances appear. I know they will appear eventually, but how soon is anyone's guess. When the time comes I will see which stocks on my list (which I share later in this book) have gone on sale. I'm keeping an eye on this new discovery, Zoom, because I believe the price will probably fall from around $82 into the $75 range, and if world events or the stock market get shaky, its possible the stock could reach the $60-$70 range. It seems like a long way from here, but the stock market can gyrate wildly.

Also, I just want to mention that while the gist of this book is picking stocks that meet all eight criteria of The TITANIUM Technique, you can be flexible. For example, I'm considering Zoom right now even though it's a relatively new company and has no moat;

there are other companies who offer video conferencing and there's no durable competitive advantage there. Also, the stock price in the $80s seems high to me, but I'm willing to be patient to see if I get a chance at lower prices. So being flexible might give me a chance to get a company when it's small, in the early part of its growth phase.

You might not know what a crash feels like

It's very hard to describe what it's like. I think I got inoculated from the emotions that cause people to panic and do really stupid things when the market crashes. I say this only from experience, because as I just explained, I was buying stocks during the financial crisis when everyone else was freaking out.

For investors just starting out, you may never have seen a bear market or even a sharp stock market decline, so you don't know how you'll respond. I think the emotional response doesn't make any sense, it's like being in a sailboat with a friend, and suddenly it starts getting windy and the waves are smashing into the side of the boat, and you're taking in water. If you lose your mind and start to freak out you're not going to help yourself out of the messy situation.

Instead you can lower your sail (or sails if there's a jib or a spinnaker). You can make sure you're wearing your life vest in case you wind up overboard. You can get your flares out and shoot some off so other boats know you're in distress. You can get on your radio (every boat must have one) and call for other nearby boats asking for help. You can call the coastguard. I'm just pointing out a number of things you can do to avert devastation and ruin, and you can save yourself and put yourself in a good position to weather the storm.

The same thing happens when the market gets dark and gloomy and all the stocks you own, and every other stock in the exchange is cratering every day. Losses of 5%, 7%, 10%, 25%, and 30% are common when stocks crash. So you have to be philosophical about it, and realize that "this too shall pass." The philosopher Spinoza said that one must look at things in the aspect of eternity[1].

I think the long term view makes a lot of sense; you're buying stocks for their benefits five, 10, or 20 years fror now — for you, and maybe for future generations of your family. So you shouldn't worry about some stock market storm today, because it will go away, and in a while it will just be a distant memory. The long-term view helps you to be ready for the big blows to the market, and it helps you to remain calm; it is essential to successful investing.

FOURTEEN

HOW TO BUY STOCKS

WHILE SOME READERS may be familiar with stock trading I thought it would be helpful to newer investors to distinguish between two ways of buying stocks. When you buy stocks you place an "order" to buy stocks, and there are two main orders I think you should now about: a buy limit order, and a market order.

I will describe both of these orders so readers can be familiar with these expressions and know how to use them[1]. If you've already traded stocks this will be very basic information, so feel free to skip over this chapter.

Let's first focus on the buy limit order, because I think this makes most sense as it offers a level of protection you don't get with a market order to buy.

A buy limit order

A buy limit order is an order to buy a stock at a specific price or lower. For example, if you want to buy Stock X and it's currently selling at $77.50 and you want to buy it at $75 you would place a *limit order to buy* 10 shares of Stock X at $75. If the price goes down to that level your order can execute, meaning it is filled by the brokerage firm and you've bought 10 shares of stock at $75 per share for a total of $750 plus any brokerage commission. A limit order can only be filled if the stock's market price reaches the limit price. While limit orders do not guarantee execution, they help ensure that an investor does not pay more than a pre-determined price for a stock.[2]

Why would you use a limit order instead of the "default" which is called a market order? Well, during the trading day stock prices can fluctuate dramatically, and we're talking on a second by second basis. Sellers may dump (sell) a large amount of stock, driving the price down, and buyers may buy a lot of stock which sends the price up sharply.

Just as there are buy limit orders, there are sell limit orders as well, and they execute at the sell limit price or higher. While they're not guaranteed to execute, they're only filled if the stock's market price reaches the limit price. They help ensure that an investor sells their stock at a pre-determined price or higher.

Market order to buy

Let's say you wanted to buy stock X and its market price was $77.50. You would log onto your trading account, place a *market order to buy* 10 shares of Stock X. You don't specify a price, and you will simply get whatever price the stock is selling for at that moment. If there is strong demand when you're about to place your order then stock price might climb quickly and you'll see that your brokerage executed your order and bought 10 shares of Stock X at $81.00 per share for a total of $810 plus any brokerage commission. You paid the market price at the current market price.

There is nothing inherently wrong with placing market orders. One of the pros is that you get immediate execution at the current price, and it's guaranteed to execute so you don't have to worry that your order won't fill. One of the cons is that you lose control over the price you pay, and if you're buying a lot of stock market fluctuations can cause you to pay a high price if the market price suddenly jumps.

I've never had a problem using market orders, but I do wish I'd known about limit orders earlier. They give you a handle on the stock price and give you a degree of control. I've noticed that experienced traders tend to use limit orders because they've witnessed or experienced bad situations where the stock buyer paid much more than expected. The best I can do is share this information with you now so at least you'll know about them.

FIFTEEN

LET'S NOT PARTY LIKE IT'S 1999

LET me help you understand a party going on back in 1999. I was an investor back then, though only through mutual funds. I didn't know about stocks at the time, but I was aware of the stock market and it had been climbing a lot. One of the hallmarks of the time was that people were starting up Internet companies, and almost any publicly traded company companies with ".com" after the name was worth hundreds of millions or billions of dollars.

Regular people who worked at those (mostly unprofitable) companies suddenly saw themselves worth millions because the value of their shares kept going up. Everything ended badly, and by the spring of 2000 the dot com crash had begun and thousands of companies crashed down to earth and went belly-up. People who were millionaires on paper just a few months earlier were suddenly looking for jobs.

It feels a little bit like 1999 right now. Not exactly the same, but the feeling that there's a lot of speculation in markets is real. Also, many investors have not yet experienced a significant market decline, and they tend to happen every now and then. Some time in the next year, or two, or three, markets will likely plunge 10% - 15% or more.

I'm not sounding a warning bell, and I'm certainly not selling my stocks in a panic. I just realize that there is a euphoria around stocks, and everybody seems to have a YouTube channel touting the latest stock du jour.

The result of all this excitement around stocks is that prices just keep going up. The value of a company is one thing, and the price of the stock of that company is completely different. Sometimes these two things become disconnected, so you have a stock that's really worth $10 selling for $20 or $30 or $50 because everyone's so excited about it. People don't want to miss the boat, so they keep buying the stock, which sends the stock price even higher.

This behavior is epitomized by companies that are not profitable but have stocks selling at high prices. Typically, a company has to start earning profits or it will go out of business. These profit-less businesses are being kept alive by cash given them to them by investors or brokerage firms just to keep them going. The company can't survive by itself; it's dependent on outside money.

It's like a really sick patient in the ICU who needs oxygen to stay alive. If you take away that oxygen they'll die. Same for these businesses that don't make a profit. The cash they're given by investors is like oxygen, and once they use it up they'll go out of business. So they try to make all that cash last long enough so they can figure things out turn a profit.

There are several companies right now who wouldn't survive without the "oxygen" provided by investors. I'll name a few: Uber, Lyft, WeWork (struggling to go public, profitless, and in trouble), Beyond Beef, etc.

During boom times like these, even the unprofitable companies float along and people are very happy and excited about them. But when shit gets real and the stock market crashes (and it will, we just don't know when) these companies will not be loved. Peoples' attitude change quickly, and suddenly these companies are in trouble. I'm not saying Uber is done — I think they'll be around for a while, because they are like a flywheel business, throwing off Uber Eats,

Uber Restaurant Partners, Uber Freight, Uber Bike, that make them look like they might just make it. Lyft does not look so fortunate, and they might just be toast before long.

Don't worry, and don't panic. Instead, look forward to the times when stocks get cheap. Have some extra money in your bank and brokerage accounts to take advantage of the low prices when they appear; no one ever regrets having some extra money around when they need it.

The stock market will give you the opportunity to buy stocks cheaply. This may happen sooner rather than later. Be prepared for these opportunities. That's the best gift I can give you; we are on a point on a curve. Whether it will go up or down is anyone's guess; when that happens, don't panic and be ready to buy the stocks you're learning about now. Remember, your willingness to buy stocks should increase as their prices fall.

AFTERWORD

Have you referred to the list you made at the start of the book? If you haven't made a list yet, now is a good time to start.

I'd like to show you the five stocks on my list. These are stocks I understand, but they don't necessarily apply to you. I'm providing this list so you'll have an example of how I decide on which stocks I'll most likely buy. Right now[1] I'm looking at these companies:

1. Adobe (ADBE
2. Illumina (ILMN)
3. Costco (COST)
4. Microsoft (MSFT)
5. Starbucks (SBUX)

In addition, I'll be watching Zoom (ZM), the video conferencing company, to see if that stock gets any cheaper. The stock closed on March 3, 2020 at $117.47. If Zoom stock entered the $50-$70 range (or below) it would be more interesting to me; in my opinion it's too expensive now.

Be sure to take your time in understanding each of your businesses – I know I will. The annual report is often the best place to start and gain firsthand knowledge. I've read about the companies listed above for several years now and have read through reams of annual reports. I'm *about* ready to invest.

There isn't one single formula that will make you rich. So stop that kind of magical thinking right now. You need to get a grasp of the important concepts, know a lot about business and human behavior, and have the right temperament — one that doesn't seek action for action's sake, and isn't trying to get rich fast.

Experiment and enjoy

Have fun with investing — the only way to improve is to put yourself out there and not be afraid of making mistakes. Because you will. When you make mistakes, just be sure to pick failure's pocket and learn something along the way.

You have unique life experiences that make you an expert in certain areas, and you'll have an enormous advantage if you stick to the businesses you understand.

The stock market can suddenly change course for totally unpredictable reasons. When you do have the occasional opportunities to buy the stock of a wonderful business run by a talented leader, that will be hog heaven day.

THANK YOU

If you enjoyed this book and feel it would be helpful to other readers, *Can I ask you for a quick favor?*

If you can find a minute today to leave a short review for *Smart Stocks* at Amazon, I would be super thankful.

This is a new book, and I hope you found it useful and learned something along the way.

As a new author, your review will help others get a feel for whether the book will be useful to them before they spend money on the purchase.

I appreciate you taking the time to leave a review, and I know future readers will too.

Thanks so much!

Jeff Luke

CONNECT

If there's anything you wish you could learn about investing but didn't find in these pages, please send me a message and I'll consider including the material in a future edition.

You can reach me by email at jlukephoto@gmail.com

Thanks for taking the time to read this book. I appreciate your time and look forward to hearing from you.

ACKNOWLEDGMENTS

I would like to thank the following people who helped bring this book to fruition. Edwin provided the artwork that graces the cover and the illustrations throughout the book.

Amadeus did exceptional work proofreading the first draft and made helpful observations that greatly improved the book. Any typos you may have found are probably the result of changes I made after he'd already done his work.

Olivia designed the cover using Edwin's artwork and her creative eye. Khunploy picked the stocks that comprised the portfolio discussed in chapter 6. Who knew, almost 10 years ago that the list of stocks she came up with in Starbucks be the basis of a real stock portfolio we could follow?

Liz was a helpful sounding board for ideas ranging from content to cover design, and provided her keen eye for writing and style.

Much gratitude to family and friends who showed enthusiasm for the fact that I'm a fanatic when it comes to learning about investing, and supported me when they had no particular interest in learning about stocks.

For everyone I know who encouraged me, looked at the book and found it useful, and to my readers who let me know this book makes a difference — thank you so much. I appreciate your generosity, it means a lot.

DISCLAIMER

Disclaimer:

The material in this book is for informational purposes only. Nothing in this book constitutes an offer or solicitation of financial advice and is not intended to provide investment, legal, tax, or other professional or financial advice.

Nothing in this book is to be construed as an offer or a recommendation to buy or sell a security. Additionally, the material in this book does not constitute a representation that the investments described herein are suitable or appropriate for any person.

Such content therefore should not be relied upon for the making of any personal financial and investment decisions. Persons accessing this information are strongly encouraged to obtain appropriate professional advice before making any investment or financial decision.

Disclosure: The author owns stock in Amazon, Berkshire Hathaway, Carmax and Waters, which were referred to in this book.

Before investing, please remember to:

1. Never invest in something that you don't understand.

2. Never invest based on anyone else's opinion.

3. Ask for assistance if you need it.

NOTES

Introduction

1. I believe that bitcoin is used as a gambling device. Just because people gamble on bitcoin does not mean cryptocurrencies are evil. I believe the blockchain presents a useful way of making transactions cheaply and anonymously, and it's important to distinguish between logging transactions and making secure payments and the buying and selling of bitcoin itself. Bitcoin itself is an asset that creates nothing, and I don't think bidding its price up higher and higher helps anyone. The blockchain itself is a useful technology.
2. A subreddit is a message board on the website reddit.com
3. New Age Corporate and Investment Acronyms: https://www.cartalk.com/radio/letter/new-age-corporate-and-investment-acronyms-1

2. Identify

1. I have been told by two of my neighbors (one next door and the other across the street) that Jimi Hendrix lived in my house for several years. His mother was addicted to drugs, so while he attended Garfield High, he spend most of his time at his aunt's house, which is the house I bought. His aunt lived with Bob Hall, the man who lived in the house before me. The house has a history that I learn about one fragment at a time from different people, all of whom are older than me, who have lived in the neighborhood during the pre-Internet era and knew Mr. Hall for many of his 100 years. I drink the water from the tap despite the presence of Brita water filters and reverse-osmosis systems, as I believe that, given his long life, whatever Mr. Hall drank was a fountain of youth.
2. After I finally found the crack, I called a company to help me patch it. The expert sent over to examine the foundation, told me that the big mystery rocks you find when digging out a trench are referred to as "dinosaur eggs" in the foundation repair and waterproofing business.
3. According to Wikipedia, falcons eat other birds while hawks and owls generally eat small mammals.
4. Garden Web: Do Hawks Eat Roadkill? https://www.gardenweb.com/discussions/2239754/do-hawks-eat-roadkill
5. Bird Eden: What Do Hawks Like to Eat? [https://birdeden.com/what-do-hawks-eat]
6. A wide economic moat is a competitive business advantage that will last a long time. It doesn't matter how much an industry is going to affect society, or how fast it will grow. What matters is determining if a company will have a competitive advantage over the others in their industry, and predicting if that advantage will

last a long time. A wide moat, like the kind around a castle, makes a business resistant to competition. We will cover moats in greater detail in chapter 8.
7. Charlie Munger said there is one other person besides Warren Buffett he entrusts with his personal wealth.
    "I'm 95 years old. I've given Munger money to some outsider to run once in 95 years," Munger said. "That's Li Lu."
    Li is the founder and chairman of Himalaya Capital a China-focused investment fund headquartered in Seattle. Munger and others have called Li the Chinese version of Warren Buffett. Both are value investors and both are wildly famous in China for their ability to generate enormous amounts of wealth. https://qz.com/work/1551328/the-only-person-besides-warren-buffett-who-charlie-munger-trusts-with-his-money/
8. The book value per share weighs stockholders' equity against shares outstanding. In other words, it represents the value of all shares divided by the number of shares issued. If you're unfamiliar with finance and accounting terms, you could say that book value is how an accountant could measure the value of the company, and over time you want that number to grow, not to remain stagnant or decline.
9. We Work Hits Jefferies Financial Group Hard https://www.fool.com/investing/2019/10/01/wework-hits-jefferies-financial-group-hard.aspx
10. This is my adaptation of "Annus Horribilus." The expression was brought to modern prominence by Queen Elizabeth II in a speech to Guildhall on 24 November 1992, marking the 40th anniversary of her accession, in which she described the year as an *annus horribilis*.[2]
    1992 is not a year on which I shall look back with undiluted pleasure. In the words of one of my more sympathetic correspondents, it has turned out to be an *annus horribilis*. https://en.wikipedia.org/wiki/Annus_horribilis
11. YouTube video titled: Warren Buffett & Charlie Munger: Diversification
12. For disclosure, as of 8/30/2019 I own shares of Amazon, Berkshire Hathaway, Carmax and Waters from this list.
13. I own stock in Amazon, Berkshire Hathaway, Carmax and Waters as of August 30, 2019
14. For disclosure, I don't yet own shares of Adobe but I do own shares of Carmax and Waters. I like all three companies, but I would like a sensible price to buy the Adobe shares, and currently they're selling for what I believe to be an inflated price.

3. Talent

1. Buffett interview with Becky Quick on CNBC.
2. BYD is an abbreviation of "Build Your Dreams" and is a company founded in 1995 by Wang Chuanfu in Shenzhen, Guangdong, China. The company began as a rechargeable-battery factory and branched out into electric cars, buses, bicycles, and most recently a monorail system called "Skyrail. The first public Skyrail line opened in Yinchuan in 2018, and by 2019, a number of cities around the world had placed orders for Skyrail systems.
3. The Water Coolest (TWC) is an online newsletter that you can have sent to your

inbox at the start of every business day. The website claims it "isn't your daddy's business journal. It's an informative and conversational morning investing newsletter that "will have you ready to snap necks and cash checks." It's a hilarious, irreverent, no-bullshit look at life on the street. https://www.thewatercoolest.com/
4. WeWork CEO returns $5.9 million the company paid him for 'We' trademark https://www.cnbc.com/2019/09/04/wework-ceo-returns-5point9-million-the-company-paid-for-we-trademark.html
5. The Water Coolest, The Headlines, September 5, 2019
6. The Water Coolest, "In Other News," September 11, 2019.
7. "One Up on Wall Street" by Peter Lynch, Fireside 2000
8. Even mediocre CEOs get huge pay packages: Vox https://www.vox.com/2014/7/23/5927165/chart-the-weak-relationship-between-ceo-pay-and-performance

4. A Sensible Price

1. For those of you who'd like to watch it, the title is "How to Pay a Fair Price for a Stock" and the video goes through the simple steps to value the Starbucks company and a sensible stock price.
2. This is the closing stock price as of September 25, 2019.

5. No

1. A subreddit is a message board on the website reddit.com
2. The Snowball: Warren Buffett and the Business of Life by Alice Schroeder, Bantam Books
3. Disclosure: As of this writing on August 28, 2019 I don't own any of these stocks.
4. Ben Graham is the author of "The Intelligent Investor" and considered the father of value investing.
5. Ben Graham Lectures: Current Problems in Security Analysis
6. To have skin in the game is an expression that means to have a personal stake in a desired outcome.
7. Robinhood is a smartphone app that lets users trade stocks with no trading commissions. Accounts are free of maintenance charges and provide an easy way to set up an account and get started for a beginning investor. Because of the ease of use, Robinhood could be a reasonable way to establish a separate account for intelligent speculation to make sure you don't mingle your speculative and investment operations in the same account.

6. Invest

1. Berkshire Hathaway Annual Shareholder Meeting. YouTube video https://www.youtube.com/watch?v=VCwIAnjAqiM
2. I say "your" businesses because you're literally a part-owner. You can proudly say that you are one of the owners of that company. You can take part in shareholder

elections and are invited to attend the annual general meeting of shareholders where the CEO and executive leadership discuss the accomplishments over the past year and talk about plans for the future.
3. Poor Charlie's Almanack: The Wit and Wisdom of Charles T. Munger. Compiled by Peter D. Kaufman
4. Adjusted for splits
5. When the stock market goes down for a short while it's called a "down leg" and if it goes up for a short while it's called an "up leg." These are terms that refer to usually a few days or weeks of trading. When I talk about a few big legs down, just think about that feeling of being in a rollercoaster when you're going along level and suddenly you drop off the edge for a breathtaking drop. That's a down leg! The stock market (mis)behaves in the same way, and just when you think things have normalized it drops off the cliff again...another down leg. Most people are freaking out during these panic times, which makes them sell, which exacerbates the freefall. Those who don't sell out during the freefall get to buy shares cheaply at the bottom!

7. Understanding

1. YouTube video - "Warren Buffett & Charlie Munger: Diversification"
2. As the manager of the Fidelity Magellan Fund between 1977 and 1990, Lynch averaged a 29.2% annual return, consistently more than doubling the S&P 500 index and making it the best-performing mutual fund in the world, according to Wikipedia. https://en.wikipedia.org/wiki/Peter_Lynch

8. Moat

1. You can always sell your stock if the business begins to falter, but the problem is that sometimes an investor will not sell because a setback seems temporary, but leads to another small problem, and another, and eventually when the time comes to sell the stock is down some awful amount and it's never coming back. Ben Franklin said "Beware of expenses. A small leak will sink a great ship" and this applies to dwindling stock prices. Gradual declines in the value of a company translate — sometimes abruptly — into a lower stock price.
2. Data from Morningstar as of August 30, 2019
3. 8 of the top 10 Smartphones on the Planet Are Made by Apple: https://www.forbes.com/sites/johnkoetsier/2018/04/18/8-of-the-top-10-most-profitable-smartphones-on-the-planet-are-made-by-apple/#1beb9f67db18
4. A survey shows that iPhone customers are not even contemplating switching brands today. In a December 2018 survey by Kantar, 90% of U.S.-based iPhone users said they planned to remain loyal to future Apple devices. Apple CEO Tim Cook on the company's 2019 Q1 earnings https://www.imore.com/apple-earnings-q1-2019
5. Huawei's phone sales are ballooning while Apple and Samsung's slump

https://www.theverge.com/circuitbreaker/2019/5/1/18525034/huawei-apple-samsung-smartphone-market-share-idc-2019
6. Jony Ive Wikipedia page: https://en.wikipedia.org/wiki/Jony_Ive
7. "The Four" by Scott Galloway - Portfolio, 2017
8. Galloway was featured on Recode Decode, hosted by Kara Swisher. Source: "What's the secret to Apple's brand? Boiled down to one word, it's sex." https://www.vox.com/2017/9/12/16290910/apple-event-iphone-x-branding-sex-scott-galloway-the-four-recode-decode-podcast-kara-swisher
9. Apple Users are Dumping iPhones and Buying Samsung https://www.zdnet.com/article/apple-users-are-dumping-iphones-and-buying-samsung/
10. Business Insider https://www.businessinsider.com/apple-iphone-more-loyal-android-chart-2017-5
11. The only people I know who own Windows phones are people who work at Microsoft. I have zero friends who walk around with Windows phones except Microsoft employees who cannot use iPhones at work for obvious reasons, and are confined to using Windows phones for work, and are iPhone users only in the privacy of their own homes (with curtains drawn).
12. Coke's Moat has More Fizz than Pepsi's" by Adam Fleck, Morningstar https://www.morningstar.com/articles/649012/cokes-moat-has-more-fizz-than-pepsis
13. Disclosure: I own shares of Berkshire Hathaway, and GEICO is a wholly-owned subsidiary of BH.
14. As of Q2 2018 only Samsung (21.0%) and Huawei (15.9%) had greater market share than Apple (12.1%) of the worldwide smartphone market. Smartphone Market Share https://www.idc.com/promo/smartphone-market-share/vendor
15. SNKRS app on Nike website https://news.nike.com/news/snkrs-app-update
16. Nike Has a New Digital Playbook—And It Starts With Sneakerheads
17. Sneaker makers like Nike and Adidas are facing a dilemma as resale is on its way to becoming a $6 billion business https://www.businessinsider.com/nike-adidas-role-sneaker-resale-market-2019-8
18. Nike vs. Adidas: The three stripes is making gains on the swoosh — but that doesn't tell the whole story https://business.financialpost.com/investing/trading-desk/nike-vs-adidas-the-three-stripes-is-making-gains-on-the-swoosh-but-that-doesnt-tell-the-whole-story
19. This is not a list of all wide-moat companies. It is a small group of companies that I understand well and I believe they possess wide moats.
20. Disclosure: As of August 30, 2019 I own shares of Amazon, Berkshire Hathaway, and Waters.
21. The inside story of why Amazon bought PillPack in its effort to crack the $500 billion prescription market https://www.cnbc.com/2019/05/10/why-amazon-bought-pillpack-for-753-million-and-what-happens-next.html

9. How to Read an Annual Report

1. NVIDIA closing stock price on September 20, 2019 was 172.69 and

10. Anatomy and Dissection of a 10-K

1. Financial analysts, like any small group of specialists, have their own vocabulary, and calling this document the "K" is part of their verbal shorthand.
2. 10-K definition from The Strategic CFO: strategiccfo.com
3. Companies with more than $10 million in assets and a class of equity securities that is held by more than 2000 owners must file a 10-K. https://en.wikipedia.org/wiki/Form_10-K
4. The annual report contains the 10-K, along with the letter to shareholders and other information about the business and its activities during the past year.
5. These analysts recommend stocks for their brokers to sell, so they're called "sell-side" analysts.
6. These analysts give recommendations about which stocks their institutions should buy, so they're called "buy-side" analysts.
7. As of market close on December 31, 2017
8. Adobe 2018 Form 10-K https://www.adobe.com/content/dam/acom/en/investor-relations/pdfs/ADBE-10K-FY18-FINAL-CERTIFIED.pdf
9. Item 1A of Illumina's 10-K lists risk factors https://www.sec.gov/Archives/edgar/data/1110803/000111080316000175/fy201510-k.htm
10. Genetics Primer included at the beginning of the Illumina, Inc. 10-K https://www.sec.gov/Archives/edgar/data/1110803/000111080316000175/fy201510-k.htm

11. Putting It All Together

1. Zoom CEO Eric Yuan on IPO: https://youtu.be/ja9VMe18sh8
2. Market capitalization refers to the total dollar market value of a company's outstanding shares. Commonly referred to as "market cap," it is calculated by multiplying a company's shares outstanding by the current market price of one share. Definition from investopedia.
3. As of October 31, 2019 there were 0.293B shares of Zoom Video Communications outstanding according to marcrotrends.net
4. Market cap is the number of shares outstanding multiplied by the current stock price.
5. https://www.barrons.com/articles/zoom-ipo-eric-yuan-crazy-valuation-stock-51555615027
6. There were 0.293B shares of Zoom Video Communications outstanding according to marcrotrends.net
7. One Up on Wall Street by Peter Lynch, Fireside, 1989. This is an excellent book about investing. Some of the examples are kind of dated because the book is from the pre-Internet era, but the approach to thinking about stocks is solid.
8. $117.47 was the closing price on March 3, 2020. By the time you read this the price will likely have changed.
9. Disclosure: As of Sept 20, 2019 I did not own shares of Zoom stock.
10. https://www.bloomberg.com/news/articles/2019-04-18/zoom-video-soars-to-16-billion-valuation-in-u-s-trading-debut

11. "Insider" is a term describing a director or senior officer of a company, as well as any person or entity that beneficially owns more than 10% of a company's voting shares.
12. Buying Instagram is probably the smartest thing Facebook has ever done. https://qz.com/1314089/instagrams-worth-is-now-estimated-to-be-100-billion/
13. Comedian Bill Burr gets credit for the skydiving analogy.
14. 109-Year-Old Veteran and His Secrets to Life Will Make You Smile. YouTube video: https://www.youtube.com/watch?v=BXyfCGDnuWs
15. Having skin in the game means having some of your own money at stake so that you're taking some risk. When you have skin in the game you tend to pay closer attention to a business.

13. Get Ready to Buy Stocks

1. Baruch Spinoza's "Sub specie aeternitatis" is an expression describing what is universally and eternally true, without any reference to or dependence upon the temporal portions of reality. From Wikipedia.

14. How to Buy Stocks

1. If readers have never before bought stocks, I recommend calling a brokerage firm for instructions, reading articles and watching YouTube videos to get a solid grasp of the basics. The limit order explained here is a relatively easy thing to do, but you should understand the basics of placing a stock trade before you get into the details of limit orders.
2. United States Securities and Exchange Commission (SEC) website - Limit Orders: https://www.sec.gov/fast-answers/answerslimithtm.html

Afterword

1. As of September 18, 2019, when this book was published.

ABOUT THE AUTHOR

Jeff Luke lives and works as a photographer and writer in Seattle, Washington. His photography has appeared in *The New York Times* and other publications worldwide.

 This is his third book about investing. Earlier books include *Stock Market Success* (2016) and *Stock Market Intelligence* (2018).

 His book "Animal Donut: Images & Stories" features artistic photos of animals & donuts: animaldonut.com and on Instagram @animaldonut

 He enjoys biking, photography, writing, and taking huskies Maximus and Snowy for romps in the snow.

 If you have any questions or would just like to connect, please email jlukephoto@gmail.com

www.ingramcontent.com/pod-product-compliance
Lightning Source LLC
Chambersburg PA
CBHW060830220526
45466CB00003B/1047